DEACONS IN THE MINISTRY OF THE CHURCH

A Report to the House of Bishops of the General Synod of the Church of England

D1102570

16377

GS 802

**This Report has the authority only
of those who prepared it**

CHURCH HOUSE PUBLISHING
Church House, Great Smith Street, London SW1P 3NZ

ISBN 0 7151 3718 2

Published January 1988 for the General Synod of the Church of England by
Church House Publishing
Second impression November 1988

Typeset by Litho Link Limited, Welshpool, UK.
Printed by The Camelot Press, Southampton, UK.

Contents

Foreword

At the beginning of 1986 we asked the Bishop of Portsmouth to prepare a report for the House of Bishops on the theology of a permanent diaconal ministry.

This Report was considered by the House at its meeting in October 1987. The House expressed great appreciation for the work the Bishop of Portsmouth had undertaken and readily agreed that the Report should be published under its authority. Although its conclusions lead to a particular understanding and present a possible model of diaconal ministry, we hope that these may contribute constructively to continuing thinking within the Church.

We shall ourselves consider further the issues the Report raises, particularly in the light of a debate upon it in the General Synod and of discussions at the Lambeth Conference.

We shall then be in a position to bring forward firm proposals, long awaited, about the future of the Diaconate.

On behalf of the House of Bishops
ROBERT CANTUAR:
Chairman

Introduction

This Report has been written in response to the request of the House of Bishops of the General Synod of the Church of England, for work to be done 'particularly on the theology of the permanent diaconate in the light of the work which was already in hand and of the experience of particular forms of specialist diaconal ministry already being established in a number of dioceses'.[1] In 1981 there had been a Private Member's motion by Mr T. L. Dye which was passed by General Synod, requesting the House of Bishops to consider the possibility of the diaconate's being 'a ministry open to men and women on a lifelong basis'.[2] More recently the Bishops had considered an ACCM Response to *Developments in the Distinctive Diaconate with Special Reference to the Portsmouth Scheme* which had been produced by a working party under the chairmanship of Bishop John Waine, then of St Edmundsbury and Ipswich.

But interest in a 'revival' of the diaconate had begun some years previously and the 1968 report *Women in Ministry* was in effect a review of diaconal ministry. Among other things it stated: 'Briefly, the Church needs to determine whether the diaconate is, or should be, an order of ministry within the clergy or not.'[3] Six years later, there was published the report of an ACCM Working Party, *Deacons in the Church*,[4] which saw no purpose either in 're-establishing' or even in retaining the diaconate, and recommended its abolition. General Synod did not endorse this recommendation in its debate in November 1977, but instead 'took note' of a further report by the Council of ACCM, *The Ministry of Deacons and Deaconesses*, which set out three options for the diaconate: 'as a short and intermediate stage through which pass all candidates for the priesthood'; its discontinuance in the Church of England; or its enlargement to include lay workers, deaconesses and others in a 'permanent' diaconate.[5]

By July 1987, more than 700 women had been ordained as deacons and the Church of England has suddenly found itself with a large number of *de facto* 'permanent' deacons. There is thus an immediate need to decide on the place of the diaconate within its life.

1

But the question of the re-establishment of the diaconate as a permanent, distinctive or vocational ministry was raised as long ago as 1878 at the Lambeth Conference by the bishops of the West Indies. It was then said to be a matter for dioceses and provinces to decide for themselves.[6] In 1958 and 1968 the Lambeth Conference passed resolutions encouraging consideration of 'a recovery of the diaconate as a significant and operative order within the sacred ministry'.[7] Following this, the ACC in Trinidad in 1976 gave positive consideration to the matter,[8] whilst in Nigeria in 1984 it stated its wish to encourage the process in which the diaconate is seen as a distinct order of servanthood ministry.[9]

This document seeks to be part of that process and is presented in three parts.

In *Part One* there is set out in some detail the history and the current practice of the churches. This is the longest part of the Report for, although much of the material is available in a number of works on the diaconate, it seemed important to gather it together, in order to provide as full a background as possible.

Of particular significance within this Part are Chapters 4 and 5, 'Diaconal Ministries in the Church of England Today', and 'The Diaconate in Ecumenical Dialogue', which give an overview of current perceptions and practice. In any rethinking of the diaconate, account has to be taken not only of the Church's tradition but also of contemporary experience. For the Holy Spirit speaks to us both through the faith and order of the past, and through the merging patterns of ministry in the Church's life today.

Part Two outlines a theology of the diaconate. It is followed in *Part Three* by a consideration of various, mostly practical, issues which put flesh on the bones of theology.

It will be seen that the chief substance of this Report is to be found in Chapter 6. However, Chapter 4 (especially Section (8), p.65) and Chapter 5 (especially Section (5) p.72) provide important background material and Chapter 7 (especially Section (1), p.103) sets out some of the implications of the theology of a distinctive diaconate. Nevertheless, for the full strength of the argument, leading to the recommendation in Chapter 9 (p.119), account needs to be taken of the document as a whole.

Throughout this Report (other than in quotation) the term 'distinctive' is used, in preference to either 'permanent' or 'vocational'. Those who are expecting to be ordained to the priesthood are referred to as 'transitional' deacons.

Warmest thanks are expressed to all who completed and returned the diocesan questionnaires: an almost 100 per cent response was most encouraging. Thanks are due to the many people who have helped with this Report. Substantial contributions have been received from Canon Dr Garry Bennett of New College, Oxford; Dr G. R. Evans of Fitzwilliam College, Cambridge; Professor W. H. C. Frend, Rector of Barnwell, Peterborough; Dame Christian Howard of Coneysthorpe, York; Deacon Sister Teresa of the Community of St Andrew; and Provost David Stancliffe of Portsmouth. Amongst others, particular mention is made of The Revd John Cobb, Canon John Colver, The Revd Kathleen Dall, The Revd Rupert Davies, The Revd Peter Gunning, Canon James Hartin, The Revd Stephen Hayes, Mr M. J. Jewell, The Revd John Paterson and Canon David Williams.

Gratitude is also expressed to the Warden and Staff of St Deiniol's Library, Hawarden, for their hospitality; and to Miss Jennifer Robinson and Mrs Libby Brice of Bishopswood for the typing and reproduction of endless documents and drafts.

Most of all, thanks and appreciation are recorded for the contribution of the co-authors of this Report: Mrs Mary Tanner, of the Board for Mission and Unity, and Canon Stephen Platten, Portsmouth Diocesan Director of Ordinands. This Report would not have been possible without them.

September 1987   + TIMOTHY PORTSMOUTH

Part One

TRADITION AND CURRENT PRACTICE

1 History of the Diaconate

(1) IN SCRIPTURE AND THE EARLY CHURCH

In Scripture

1 The New Testament evidence for the origins of the ordained ministry is fragmentary and comes from different periods and different geographical regions. Nevertheless, it is clear that the New Testament does not picture a shepherdless flock. The key concept is that of a ministry of the whole people of God in which particular ministries find their place, as part of a coherent whole. By baptism all the people of God receive a status which is given by divine grace. But not all have the same specific role, nor are the general ministry and the specific ministries in tension.

2 Although there is no unified pattern of church order to be found in the New Testament, it is possible to detect a development of ideas and practice between the earlier and the later writings. Furthermore, there is some convergence between a development that is already discernible within the New Testament and that development which appears in early writings, in the Didache, 1 Clement and Ignatius of Antioch. It appears that by about A.D.110 a threefold ministry of bishop, presbyter and deacon had taken a decisive hold in Syria and Asia Minor. Soon it is found as the general pattern.

3 All three words, *episkopos, presbuteros* and *diakonos,* are found in the New Testament. As with *presbuteros* and *episkopos,* the New Testament presents us with a terminological difficulty in the case of deacons (*diakonoi*). These titles, all used for ministers with special responsibilities in the community, are not used with demonstrable consistency, or as technically exact terms. However, the word *diakonia* simply means 'service' and all ministry is service, so that, for example, the theme of 2 Corinthians is that apostleship is supremely *diakonia.*

4 Acts 6. 1–6 tells of the appointment of seven men to 'serve tables', in order to leave the Twelve Apostles free to devote themselves to prayer and to the ministry of the word. The Seven were set aside by prayer and laying-on of hands, just as Paul and Barnabas would be

commissioned for their mission (Acts 13.3). Although these seven have often been seen as the genesis of deacons, it is hard to support this from the rest of the New Testament evidence. The subsequent ministry described in Acts of two of them (Stephen and Philip) resembles the ministry of the apostles themselves rather than what came to be understood as the ministry of deacons.

5   The first mention of deacons by name occurs in Paul's letter to the Philippians (*c* A.D.60), where Paul greets the 'bishops and deacons' of the community (Phil. 1.1). In the Pastorals (*c* A.D.75), there is mention of deacons at Ephesus and it is emphasised that good conduct, sound management of affairs, and faith are required of deacons as well as of bishops (1 Tim. 3.8–13).

6   Women were admitted to diaconal office. 'The women in like manner' are mentioned in the middle of the charge to deacons in 1 Timothy, and in Rom. 16.1, Phoebe is called *diakonos*. The feminine form *diakonissa* is not found before the fourth century and even then, as well as later, we meet the form 'woman deacon' (*gune diakonos*). The enclosed character of feminine life, especially in the Levant, made deaconesses indispensable for the Church's mission there. A mosaic shows that already by *c* A.D.200 'upper class' women wore the veil in Syria.

In the Post-Apostolic and Patristic Period

7   The distinctive task for which the Seven were commissioned in Acts was one of practical service. This developed along two lines, the liturgical and the adminstrative, and as early as the patristic period the two aspects seem to have become in some measure separated. On the one hand the 'service at table' developed towards other material responsibilities in the Church, such as administering the finances of the community; this was a duty which could involve the handling of large sums of money and which required a degree of seniority, so that in practice it was impossible for a senior member of the community to be regarded as its lowliest minister. On the other hand, this service expanded and began to include a duty of service at the altar. In the time of Justin Martyr (*c*100–*c*165) deacons were taking the consecrated bread to church members who were sick or in prison and there is a strong tradition in Tertullian that deacons are called *ad altaris ministerium*. Ambrose stated that the deacon ordinarily administered the chalice (*De Officiis* i.205), whilst in the instructions

8

given by Hippolytus (3rd century) for ordaining a deacon the ordination prayer itself stresses liturgical function (Dix, pp.17f). It is also worth noting from the same instructions the relationship of the deacon to the bishop: 'when a deacon is ordained, let the bishop alone lay on his hands, for the reason that he is but for serving the bishop, to do those things which are commended by him . . .' (pp.15f).

8   The growing responsibility of deacons in the ministry of the Church is attested *c*100 by the writer of 1 Clement: 'They (the Apostles) preach from district to district, and from city to city, and they appointed their first converts, testing them by the Spirit, to be bishops and deacons of the future believers' (1 Clem. 42.4). In the Shepherd of Hermas (*c*120) deacons are placed alongside 'apostles, bishops and teachers' as those who 'serve the elect of God' (Vis. iii.5.1). So too Polycarp writes in the middle of the second century to the Church at Philippi in terms which suggest that presbyters and deacons are responsible within the administration of the Church. 'Wherefore it is necessary to refrain from all these things, and to be subject to the presbyters and deacons as to God and Christ, (*Phil.* 5.3).

9   By the end of the second century the administrative aspect of the deacon's work was enlarged, as the Church expanded in numbers and importance and acquired property in its own right. We hear (*c*200) that Callistus the 'deacon' has been put in charge of 'the catacomb' by Pope Zephyrinus, whilst in the late sixth century Gregory the Great still made substantial use of deacons in administration, in the vast papal land-holdings in Sicily and North Africa. It should be noted that the prime object of these land-holdings was to provide alms for the poor and destitute. In many patristic texts *diakonia* simply means responsibility for getting alms to the needy, a duty especially laid on the shoulders of deacons. After the Gothic wars of Justinian (6th century) and then the Lombard invasion of Italy, Gregory the Great was able to use every penny for the relief of homeless and impoverished folk, rather than use the income to line his own pocket.

10   Consonant with the trust thus placed in senior deacons was the use of deacons as ambassadors. Cyprian (d.258) sent deacons as emissaries to distant bishops in mid-third century North Africa and the deacon Rogatian takes letters to Firmilian of Cappadocia on the rebaptism issue (Letter 75.1). Later the Pope included a deacon, together with a bishop and a priest, as one of his legates to the Council (*Latrocinium*) of Ephesus in 449.

11   There was a clear intention of maintaining continuity with the spirit of Acts 6, and Rome itself was governed during the interregnum of 250–251 by 'presbyters' and 'deacons', with seven deacons each having charge of one of the seven administrative regions into which the city had been divided. As the work increased, further help was needed. So Eusebius (*HE* vi.43.11) gives evidence of the existence of seven subdeacons in Rome in 251, in order to ensure the maintenance of 1500 widows and 'other poor persons' on the Church's roll.

12   There is some evidence of trouble resulting from the increasing responsibilities of deacons for church finance and their desire to have a more prominent liturgical role. As administrators under the bishop of the considerable meals-on-wheels service provided for the indigent, deacons were influential people. They also had the task of keeping order in church when the building was (perhaps commonly) crowded, so that some physical stamina was required. Ambrosiaster comments sharply on the tensions in Rome between deacons and presbyters in the time of Pope Damarus (366–84), whilst the Council of Arles in 314 had already stated, 'concerning deacons, who we have ascertained make the offering in many places, we decree that this must cease' (16th Canon). In addition, the 18th Canon of Nicaea had ordered deacons not to get above themselves (e.g. by giving the Eucharist to presbyters), 'whereas neither canon nor custom allows that they who have no authority to offer should give the Body of Christ to those who do offer'.

13   For what we may call 'career deacons' the diaconate was in principle seen to be permanent. But two developments militated against its becoming so universally. As early as the time of Ignatius of Antioch (d. *c* 107), we find a hint of a threefold ministry, hierarchically arranged. In his letters deacons are classed as the third grade of the ministry, associated with the bishop and presbyter in serving the altar at the Eucharist (*Philadelphians* 4). At the same time, it was common to compare bishop, priest and deacon with the three Old Testament orders of high priest, priest and levite, as attested first by Clement (1 Clem.40). The second development was a tendency for deacons to succeed their bishops so that, for example, Callistus the deacon succeeded Pope Zephyrinus as Pope (218–22) over the head of the presbyter Hippolytus. In Rome and Carthage by the fourth century, the chief or 'arch' deacon was tending to become the automatic successor to the bishop.

14   This did not necessarily involve the deacon's proceeding to the priesthood some time beforehand, but we hear of deacons progressing through what were coming to be recognised as clerical grades (Cyprian, Letter 55.8). A key event in encouraging the shift to thinking of the diaconate as a stepping stone to the priesthood was the disciplinary measure of Pope Siricius (384–99) when he gave instructions that no one should be ordained deacon under the age of 30, presbyter under 40 or bishop under 50 (Letter 1.13). In 393 the Catholic African Council of Hippo relaxed the ruling and allowed the ordination of deacons at 25 (Canon 1). It gradually became usual for a deacon in the West to seek 'promotion' to the presbyterate at the age of 30, although the tradition of a permanent diaconate for senior career deacons continued.

15   Some differences between East and West are noticeable as the Greek and Latin communities began to drift apart. In the East there seems to have been less pressure for the deacon to seek 'promotion', and there was no canonical requirement for a bishop to pass through the entire range of clerical grades. But we find in the East, as in the West, deacons as senior administrators, heads of a clerical secretariat, persons of prestige and influence. A prime example was Aetius, archdeacon of Constantinople at the time of Chalcedon in 451, and responsible for much of the organisation of the Council. But the work of 'serving tables' continued in the liturgy.

16   The continuance of women deacons is attested by Pliny in his letter to Trajan in 112, where he speaks of two 'ancillae quae ministrae dicebantur' (*Letter* x.96.8). It is probable that the Greek word implied is *diakonos* but possible (if unlikely) that it is *diakonissa*. The performance of certain diaconal functions by deaconesses is well-attested in the early Church, especially in the care of the poor and sick. Until adult baptism gave way generally to infant baptism in the West in the early fifth century, women had an essential liturgical role in the baptism of women (for reasons of propriety). But their position was anomalous, for 'promotion' to the priesthood was not open to them and the social customs of the period prevented their proceeding to senior administrative office.

(2) IN THE MEDIEVAL CHURCH

17   The liturgical function of the diaconate had been of considerable scope in patristic times and it became the staple work of deacons

throughout the Middle Ages. The Eucharist was central and the deacon's office was to take care of the vessels, to receive the people's offerings and to present them to the priest (who offered them to God at the altar) and, in some churches, to read the Gospel. Deacons distributed both elements, but normally only to the people, not to any priests present. Deacons could lead the congregation's prayers; in some places they were allowed to baptise and, with episcopal permission, they could preach. In cases of extreme necessity they could reconcile penitents and they also had disciplinary authority in the local church. Of these duties, Ps.-Jerome (probably seventh century) mentions only those connected with the Eucharist. Ps.-Isidore (*Epistola ad Leudefredum*, probably of the ninth century) gives a similar but fuller list, again of tasks connected with the celebration of the Eucharist.

18   The Eucharistic theme is developed by the continuator of Aquinas' *Summa Theologiae* in an account of the respective roles of priests, deacons and subdeacons in the liturgy. All three must be celibate because those who touch holy things must be pure and holy (ST III Supple.Q.37 a.3). The priest has to do with the consecrated elements directly; the deacon as they are contained in the vessels; the subdeacon with the vessels only (ibid.a.3 ad 5). It is for this reason that at this date the priest alone might distribute the consecrated bread and the deacon might administer only the chalice, so that he touched not Christ but the vessel in which he is contained. The subdeacon took over the work of serving the Mass and washing the vessels, which in an earlier period had fallen to the deacon (ibid.). All this depends on the contemporary understanding of the doctrine of transubstantiation.

19   The place of the subdeacons was anomalous. Gregory VII enlarged the class of those on whom celibacy was enjoined to include not only deacons but subdeacons (together with monks, in whose case orders were not in question). The Lateran Council of 1139 did the same. The theologians of the Council of Trent set out the difficulty about the position of subdeacons and made a clear distinction between bishops, priests and deacons (of whom mention is made in Scripture) and subdeacons, acolytes, exorcists and so on, whose offices are acknowledged to be the Church's creation. But it was conceded that some Fathers and Councils included the subdeacons among the major orders (1563, Session 23, Chapter 2). The reformers

in general pressed for the abolition of non-Scriptural orders and Wyclif, in the *De Gradibus Cleri Ecclesiae* (pp.142–3) argues that the Bible warrants only two: deacons and priest-bishops, pointing out that different offices do not make it necessary to multiply orders to perform them. Beza, however, allowed subdeacons (II Whitgift 332, 433).

20   There seems to be no dispute in the medieval period that the diaconate proper is an order. It is commonplace to find the deacons derived from the Levites of the Old Testament (e.g. Ps.-Jerome, col. 153; Peter Lombard Sent. IV Dist. 24.10.1; Bonaventure In Sent. IV.24). Everywhere they are paired with, and distinguished from, priests. In the prayer of consecration used in the Roman liturgy of the fifth and the sixth centuries there is no reference to priestliness in the case of deacons but an emphasis instead on the variety of the gifts of ministry. Peter Lombard notes the practice by which only the bishop lays hands on the deacons, in contrast to the practice in ordaining priests. He insists that they are not co-priests but designed *ad ministerium* (Sent. IV Dist. 24.10.4). This emphasis was necessary because in many areas of rights and duties the two orders were alike. The Council of Constantinople (869–70, XXIII and XXVI) links the two orders in providing that no priest or deacon is to hold services *in aliena ecclesia* and also in discussing their respective rights of appeal to higher authority in disputes. Priests and deacons might both be licensed to preach and, again, priests and deacons are coupled in the Wycliffite Articles condemned at the Council of Constance (1415, no. 12). In the Ps.-Jerome Letter *De Septem Ordinibus Ecclesiae* it is argued that the *officia* of priest and deacon are inter-dependent and complementary, the one needing the other as there can be no rich without the poor, no poor without the rich (col.154).

21   Senior deacons, of the sort employed by Gregory the Great to administer papal estates, continued to have a place in assisting diocesan bishops. In the ninth century such deacons exercised a disciplinary role and supervised the clergy of the whole or part of a diocese, as well as administering Church property. In the custom of regarding an archdeacon as the bishop-presumptive in succession there is an implied acceptance of the diaconate as an equal but distinct ministry, alongside and parallel with that of the priesthood (cf. paras. 10 and 23). In the East it was necessary for the Council (633) and the Synod (692) of Trullo to emphasise that the diaconate is

lowlier than the priesthood. Nevertheless, there was never any real confusion on this point and we find senior deacons being ordained priest before their elevation to the episcopate.

22 Vestiges of diaconal work by women are found until the eleventh or twelfth centuries, although the canons of sixth-century Gothic councils deplore the actions of bishops who have ordained women to the diaconate, on the grounds of 'feminine physical fragility'. Whilst Peter Abelard (in his sermon on St Stephen) expressly affirms that deacons and deaconesses share in a single diaconal order, Bonaventure explains that deacons receive a *potestas* by the imposition of hand and are ordained, whilst deaconesses receive only a *benedictio* (In Sent. 24). When the office of deaconess was revived in modern times, it was not generally regarded as an order and thus there was made a separation between office and order in the role of the deaconess.

(3) IN THE CHURCH OF ENGLAND FROM THE REFORMATION

23 At the time of the break with Rome in the sixteenth century the Church of England gave little serious attention to a reform of the Order of Deacons and, in large measure, continued medieval usage. This is not, perhaps, surprising in the light of the remark of one of the bishops at Trent in 1562 that the diaconate had become an office largely stripped of its ancient functions. He thought the Council should do something about it, but was not heeded. The office continued in the Church of England because it is in Scripture and because the threefold ministry is a sign and instrument of ministerial continuity in catholic tradition. To this day Anglicans share with Roman Catholics a certain unclarity about the functions now attached to the office. The pre-Reformation deacon was a 'clerk in Holy Orders' committed to life-long celibacy and to the daily recitation of the Divine Office; he had an 'indelible character'. Though he was not a priest, it was clear that he was in 'Major Orders', unlike a subdeacon, about whom there was some doubt, or acolytes, exorcists, lectors and doorkeepers, who were in 'Minor Orders'. A deacon had a traditional liturgical role in singing the Gospel at Mass, assisting the priest at the altar and leading the prayers of the people, though usually these functions were performed by priests vested as deacons.

24   In medieval usage most ordinands remained deacon for a very short time, not more than a few weeks, before being ordained priest. When the Church laid such great emphasis on the celebration of the Mass, giving absolution after confession, and the blessing of people and objects, the priesthood was seen as the primary ministry. There was, however, an important group of clerks who remained deacon for long periods, or permanently. They were persons of some importance with a specialised function which was thought difficult to combine with the full ministerial obligations of the priesthood; they were the academics who were fellows of colleges, ecclesiastical lawyers, and royal servants engaged in an onerous work of administration or diplomacy. Such deacons could be beneficed, if they employed a priest to exercise the cure of souls, and they could also perform the work of an archdeacon. It was quite usual for eminent deacons to be nominated to a bishopric and to be ordained priest immediately before episcopal consecration.

25   The framers of the new Ordinal of 1550 seem to have accepted the medieval pattern. They had little knowledge of the early history of the ministry and their principal concern was to revise the Pontifical to exclude what in Protestant eyes were its 'superstitious' aspects. In particular, they wished to make it clear that prayer and the laying on of hands were the essential 'matter' of ordination rather than the many ceremonies of the Pontifical which involved the 'tradition' of the emblems of office. They seem to have been only marginally affected by the attempts of Continental Reformers to create a new kind of diaconate.

26   In Lutheran areas deacons were either abolished or reduced to a lay function as parish clerks or vergers. In Martin Bucer's Strassburg, deacons were parish officers concerned with charity, visiting the sick and relieving the poor. In Calvin's Geneva the deacons formed one of the four orders of ministry, below pastors, teachers and elders. Calvin based his view of them on 1 Tim. 5.9–10, and confined their work to charity. In most Calvinistic countries the diaconate was regarded as a hard and laborious work concerned with poorhouses, hospitals and orphanages.

27   The Ordinal of 1550 shows traces of this Reformed influence, derived from Bucer's *De Ordinatione Legitima* of 1549 and perhaps from the 1543 edition of Calvin's *Institutes*. The Ordinal seeks to place the deacon in a parochial context as a ministerial assistant to a parish

priest; it gives him a special ministry to the poor, but it makes it clear that he is thought of as a clerk, a preacher (if he has the bishop's permission) and a candidate for full orders after a year's probation.

28   A deacon after the Elizabethan settlement was, then, a clerk in Holy Orders rather than the holder of a lay office. With the disappearance of all the minor orders, ordination as a deacon became the way by which a man joined the ranks of the clergy; he assumed clerical dress and in the conduct of public worship his vesture was indistinguishable from that of a priest; he was obliged to say morning and evening prayer either publicly or privately. At a time when the Holy Communion was celebrated only three or four times a year and when the practice of private confession was virtually disused, a deacon could perform most of the Church's services. Indeed it was not until 1662 that the Act of Uniformity made it clear that a deacon could not be instituted to a benefice.

29   In the seventeenth and eighteenth centuries the time which a man served in the diaconate varied greatly. The Prayer Books of 1559 and 1662 stated as a norm that a deacon should continue in that state for a full year. This was, however, widely disregarded. In the parochial ministry there were very few assistant curates (at this time called readers), and most men were appointed directly to the sole charge of a parish on ordination, either as incumbents or as curates acting in the place of an absent incumbent. Thus it was usual practice for the two orders of deacon and priest to be conferred by bishops at the same time or within a few days of each other. Only those who were under age for the priesthood or who were felt to need the stimulus of a further examination were required to serve the full year. In the eighteenth century, episcopal visitations searched out curates who had failed to proceed to the priesthood and occasionally discovered men who had been deacons for many years, either because of the fees involved or because they feared an examination by the bishop's chaplains.

30   There were, then, very few deacons at any one time – with the one exception of those at the universities. Fellows of colleges filled their statutory obligation to enter into Holy Orders by being ordained to the diaconate but often did not proceed to the priesthood until they wished to leave the university for a benefice. Colleges, which had only a single service of Holy Communion a term and were served by chaplains, did not need many priests.

31   This state of things ended in the nineteenth century. Fellows of colleges were relieved of the obligation to enter into Holy Orders, and few were ordained. But the chief cause of change was the rise of the large urban parish where an incumbent needed the assistance of many 'curates'. With the rise of a new sense of professionalism in the clergy the pattern emerged of time at a theological college followed by an apprenticeship as a deacon in a training parish and a further period as a 'curate', before being thought ready to undertake the responsibility of an incumbency. The result was that the diaconate was revived but in the single form of being a year during which an apprentice learned his professional duties.

32   The revision of the Ordinal of the Church of England in the 1980 Alternative Service Book gives more definite direction to the office and work of a deacon. This is effected through the choice of the lections and in the form of the Declaration. The prayer of the Bishop before the laying-on of hands places more stress on a ministry of service than is the case in the Book of Common Prayer, and in the section following service and teaching are the key-notes, whilst in that for priests they are offering spiritual sacrifices, pronouncing absolution and proclaiming the gospel. The ministry of preaching is firmly fixed within the description of the office of the deacon and is no longer dependent upon a specific licensing by the Bishop to that ministry. There is also a clear statement of the deacon's empowering and enabling role as an ordained minister within the whole Church, encapsulated within the phrase 'to work with its [the Church's] members in caring for the poor, the needy, the sick, and all who are in trouble'. The reference to the 'inferior office' of the deacon has been excluded, as also has the implication that all deacons will be called to 'higher Ministries' in the Church.

33   These latter phrases occur in the Book of Common Prayer Ordinal in the post-communion Collect. As a result of recent Synod legislation, it must be omitted when the BCP service is being used to ordain women to the diaconate. Again, the implication is that candidates may remain in the order of deacons and need not necessarily be ordained as priests. This is in contrast to the idea, commonly held, that a deacon is but a young and inexperienced clergyman, although the revived order of deaconesses for long bore witness to the diaconate as a distinctive and permanent ministry.

17

(4) WOMEN'S MINISTRY IN THE CHURCH OF ENGLAND[10]

34 The nineteenth century in England saw many changes in the Church and amongst them was the revival of interest in the ministry of women. It is clear from the New Testament that women had a recognised place in the work of the Church and there were deaconesses in both East and West until the eleventh century. Thereafter women's ministry continued within religious orders, in England until the dissolution of the monasteries.

35 Not surprisingly, then, renewal in the Church of England began with the foundation of a sisterhood by Dr Pusey in 1845, for work in Park Village, London. A few years later was founded the Community of St Mary the Virgin at Wantage and within a few years there were no fewer than twenty communities in different parts of England. It was estimated in 1878 that at least 700 women belonged to religious orders. After initial suspicion and hostility the restoration of the religious life was accepted by the Church and formally approved at the 1897 Lambeth Conference. There followed a period of growth, with existing communities increasing in size and expanding overseas, and new communities coming into being. By 1970 there were some forty women's communities in, or associated with, the Church of England and they provided the largest number of women in full-time ministry.

36 Whilst the basis of the religious congregation is a life of prayer in community under rule, many undertook an active ministry in such fields as nursing, teaching and various kinds of social welfare. It was their devoted work among the poor and under-privileged which largely led to their acceptance by the Church in the early days. Whilst they did not consciously describe their work as diaconal, that is what it was.

37 But there was one community which did have such an aim and that was the Community of St Andrew, founded in 1861 by Elisabeth Ferard with the support of Bishop Tait of London. Its members were to be both religious and deaconesses, to work within diocesan and parochial systems.

38 The motivation for the restoration of the ministry of deaconesses was not so much the desire to revive an ancient tradition, nor perhaps to provide an outlet for the gifts of an increasing number of women

frustrated by lack of opportunities in society, but the desperate need presented to the Church by the rapidly growing urban areas. The existing parochial system could not cope with the migration to the towns of vast numbers of people in the aftermath of the Industrial Revolution, which brought much squalor, sickness and human degradation. It was not enough to provide more clergy and more church buildings, and both Bishop Tait and Bishop Thorold of Rochester (which then included Southwark) championed the cause of women's ministry as providing the means for home visiting and pastoral care.

39   A great influence on those responsible for the restoration of the ministry of deaconesses was the Kaiserswerth Institution, founded in 1836 by Pastor Fliedner in Germany. By 1861 this already had 220 deaconesses, 120 probationers and 83 outstations. Whilst not a religious community as such, it was a Christian organisation of women trained for the care of the sick and the poor, for teaching neglected children and for parish work. A deaconess was admitted to her office in a service which included laying-on of hands by the pastor. No formal vows were made, though the deaconess was expected to serve for at least five years and it was assumed that most would remain for life.

40   The Order of Deaconesses was revived in the Church of England when in 1862 Dr Tait ordained Elisabeth Ferard as a deaconess. A year later she was joined in the North London Deaconess Institution by two more, with six candidates and eight assistants. Two other dioceses followed suit; in 1867 the diocese of Chester established a house in Liverpool and in the same year the Bishop of Ely admitted the first deaconess for St Peter's, Bedford. By 1917 a further eleven institutions or houses had been established and in 1927 the Central House for the Order of Deaconesses was founded at Hindhead, providing, until it closed in 1976, a 'centre for the whole Order, with which all deaconesses can be in touch'.

41   The Church's recognition of the Order came from the Lambeth Conference in 1897, although it was not until 1923 that it was formally restored by the Convocation of Canterbury and in 1925 by that of York. It was constituted by the Resolutions of Convocation in 1939–41 and by Canons D 1–3, 1964. With the passing of the Deacons (Ordination of Women) Measure in 1986 and with the ordination by bishops of deaconesses and other women to the order of deacon, there

will be no further admissions to the Order of Deaconess, and only those members who have not been ordained deacon remain in the Order.

42 The position of the Order was never definitely clarified with respect to the status of its members. Whilst the commission on the ministry of women, preparatory to the 1920 Lambeth Conference, gave as its opinion that the ordination of a deaconess conferred Holy Orders on her, this is not stated in the Conference Resolutions. However, some deaconesses who were ordained between 1920 and 1930 certainly believed themselves to have been admitted to the third order of ministry and were understandably hurt when the special committee of the Lambeth Conference in 1930 denied the deaconess and the deacon to be equivalent in Order, stating the Deaconess Order to be *sui generis*. On the other hand, the Archbishops' Commission on the Ministry of Women referred in 1935 to the Order of Deaconesses as 'a holy order' and the 1939–41 Convocation Resolutions make use of the word 'ordination' and speak of 'a distinctive and permanent status in the Church' thereby given to the deaconess. The reluctance to use the word 'ordination' came later.

43 Obviously such ambivalence raises some sharp questions about the meaning of ordination, and has created much frustration. It will have contributed to the somewhat guarded way in which many in the Church have viewed the ministry of deaconesses, although some inside and most people outside the Church have assumed the deaconess to be a 'full' minister of the Church.

44 Liturgically, the functions of the deaconess have coincided with those of the deacon for less than twenty years. It was only in 1973 that she was allowed to undertake the customary diaconal role in the Eucharist, as well as to officiate at baptisms, funerals and the Churching of Women. From a few years previously she was allowed to preach at public worship, provided it was not at the Holy Communion, although she had previously been permitted to read Morning and Evening Prayer. For much of the time of the Order her preaching and teaching ministry was to be to women and children only, and then only at meetings or services held outside the church building.

45 Some space has been given to a sketch of the Deaconess Order because of its obvious link (and now continuity) with the ministry of

deacons. However, in addition to members of religious communities and the Deaconess Order, there are other women who in the past hundred years have exercised diaconal ministry, mostly without liturgical functions and without the direct responsibility to a bishop which was generally true of both nuns and deaconesses.

46 For women have for long given voluntary service to the Church and so have laid the foundations for full-time lay ministry. In 1857 Mrs Ranyard founded a group of Bible Women in London 'to supply the very poorest of the population with copies of the Bible and also to improve their temporal condition'. Mothers' Meetings were held and some of the Bible Women received elementary nursing training. As well as other, mostly 'religious', nursing institutions which came into being for work among the poor at this time, there were other movements which recruited from the poor to become missionaries to the poor. Their work was organised on a parochial basis and much of it was long ago absorbed by Boards or Councils of Women's Work, and so rooted in the dioceses.

47 The ministry of the Accredited Lay Worker has been largely that of pastoral assistance in the parish, although increasingly in recent years she has been involved in sector ministries (chaplaincy in education, industry, hospitals, etc., as well as holding diocesan posts). Parish ministry has involved her in visiting in home and hospital, looking after Sunday schools, helping with baptism and confirmation preparation, running organisations for children and maybe women too. Only within the last thirty years or so has she been permitted a part in liturgical worship and latterly her role has been largely identical to that of a deaconess, except that the deaconess may be authorised to baptise in the absence of the priest. Thus, in qualifications and function, there is little to distinguish the lay worker from the deaconess. It should be noted that women were admitted to the office of Reader in 1969 and an increasing proportion of Readers in training today are women.

48 An obviously diaconal ministry to the world was exercised by distinguished groups of women who have their roots in the pioneering work of Josephine Butler. The Church's Moral Welfare (later Social) Workers have sought to provide for the needs of people with problems of many kinds and have mostly been employed on a diocesan basis. Since the implementation of the 1968 Seebohm Report their role has

21

largely been exercised by Local Authorities. That they were not always accepted and understood by the Church, in spite of holding the bishop's licence, is suggested by one senior worker who in 1967 wrote '[we] are often frustrated by the disregard of the Church for our responsibility in ministry. It seems that, having won the battle for recognition by social work, we are fast losing it in the Church.'

49   Not to be forgotten in any survey of the last hundred years is the work of the Church Army and of its sisters in particular. The first training centre for women was opened in 1887 and the first women to be commissioned were known as Church Army nurses. Although founded for primarily evangelistic purposes, the Church Army's activities have included social and moral welfare work in cities, new housing areas, caravan sites and prisons. Residential care is provided for all kinds of people in need, but most of its workers are parish-based and involved in pastoral work. Its officers see themselves as lay people and many find a vocation within the society for life. A commission which reported in 1968 notes that

> the parochial sisters tend to receive more official recognition from the Church than the captains. The reason for this is that they are part of a larger ministry of women. In spite of the opportunities for evangelism which most of the sisters find in their work, many of them are dissatisfied with the scope which women workers as a whole are given at present in the ministry of the Church.

50   Finally, mention should be made of the very many women who undertook pioneering and effective ministry in the Church overseas. The Church Missionary Society sent its first woman missionary to Sierra Leone in 1820 and in 1857 the Society for the Propagation of the Gospel sent Miss Sarah Coombes to Labuan.

51   The picture which emerges is of a tremendous variety of work being undertaken by women over the past 150 years, much of it pioneered by individuals but gradually becoming centralised or ordered. There was a discernible increase in the liturgical role of women during this century, and especially since World War II. It may well be that this has contributed to a shift of emphasis in women's ministry from a diaconal ministry to those outside the Church, in pioneering days, to one which is now exercised primarily within the Church.

2 The Diaconate in the Churches

(1) THE ORTHODOX AND ORIENTAL CHURCHES

52 In the Orthodox Church there is a long tradition of the distinctive diaconate and only with the comparatively recent shortage of priests in a *diaspora* situation has there developed the use of a transitional diaconate. It is not unusual, for example, for the priest in a monastery to be chosen for ordination from among the lay brothers, in spite of there being at least one deacon in the monastery among them. An additional factor may be that the minimum age for priesthood is five years above that for the diaconate (as it was in the Western Church in the early Middle Ages). Most of all, however, it seems likely that the continuing distinctiveness of the diaconate is largely the consequence of a general resistance to change in the Orthodox tradition and the survival of the culture and language of an earlier age, the 'golden age' of the diaconate.

53 The functions of the deacon continue to be almost wholly liturgical and, indeed, such theological writing as there has been about the diaconate has been almost entirely in liturgical commentaries. He is the go-between in the Liturgy between the bishop (or priest) and the laity, giving almost all the directions, including those to the president, and where necessary he might even intervene physically to maintain order. It is the deacon who moves about the church and his voice predominates for the audible parts of the service, whether in speaking or chanting (many of the president's prayers being said *sotto voce*). He has in the Liturgy a prominent and established role.

54 However, the relationship of some deacons to the bishop in the Liturgy often extends into their being part of the bishop's household as personal assistants to the bishop himself. Thus the deacon will serve practically as well as liturgically and, depending on his ability, he might be involved in anything from fetching a suitcase to drafting letters and writing speeches. An ageing bishop (there is no retirement) would depend more and more upon his deacon for everyday tasks. In

addition to such administrative *diakonia*, there is the vestigial trace of it in the 'the great archdeacons' of the Ecumenical Patriarchate at Istanbul and they are true deacons, not priests.

55 Although the diaconate exercises little by way of a social role, the Orthodox Church does undertake a ministry of caring where it is possible for it to do so. From 1503 to the present day in Constantinople (and from 1503 to 1821 in Greece) the clergy have been barred from undertaking any kind of social service, as they are in those Balkan and Slavic churches under communist rule. However, in Greece a major church department under the Holy Synod is named *Apostoliki Diakonia* and is a kind of 'home mission' department, chiefly producing publications for parishes and, until recently, with a school for training church social workers under its jurisdiction.

56 Most dioceses in Greece have two organisations: 'Spiritual *Diakonia*' for diocesan preachers, confessors, publications, libraries and schools of church music; and 'Philanthropic *Diakonia*' for orphanages, old people's homes and special schools. An interesting example of serving ministry is found at Kalyviani in Crete where Bishop Timotheos established a 'social-serving' village consisting of a women's monastery, orphanages, schools, hostels, a craft-training centre, a residence for the disabled elderly and a conference and retreat centre.

57 Canonical provision for deaconesses and their role in the baptism of women has not been revoked, but they seem to have disappeared in the Orthodox church at the end of the twelfth century, with the coming of Arab (and, later, Latin and Turkish) domination. Given the ruthlessness of Islam towards converts to Christianity, there was good reason for making no mention of even the existence of deaconesses. However, the absence of documentation does not prove that they did not continue or that new ones were not ordained to meet local needs.

58 In Russia in 1906 Grand Duchess Elizabeth Feodorovna tried to form a deaconess order, with proposals which included ordination (with stole) by a bishop, for work in parishes. These were vetoed by the Council of the Russian Orthodox Church and she founded, instead, a nursing order. She was buried in Gethsemane where the Orthodox Church in Exile venerates her as a 'new martyr'. Her niece Princess

Andrew of Greece (Alice of England) followed her example in the 1940s by seeking to form a Greek nursing order of nuns.

59   Another modern 'saint', highly venerated, was Metropolitan Nektarios of Pentapolis who contributed to the restoration of the diaconate by ordaining two nuns as deaconesses in 1911. They wore the *orarion* (stole) and diaconal cuffs and assisted the priest at the altar by preparing it for the Liturgy. Although they did not take the deacon's part in the Liturgy, they carried the Holy Communion to those sisters unable to be present. Bishop Nektarios' action was condemned by some who objected to the two women's functioning as deaconesses, describing them instead as subdeaconesses. Nevertheless, his successor as Director of Rizareion Ecclesiastical School, Archbishop Papadopolos of Athens, ordained eight nuns in the mid 1930s.

60   Also in Athens was the foundation in 1952/54 of the St Barbara Deaconess College. Until its amalgamation with other institutions in 1985, its graduates served the Church as social workers, but the bishops would not ordain them as deaconesses. To this day, in spite of Consultations in 1976 (Agapia) and 1983 (Middle East Council of Churches), no leading Orthodox bishop publicly supports any action being taken to restore the Order of deaconesses.

61   There is a real sense in which *diakonia* is in fact exercised by the bishop, as he responds to personal appeals made to him, often from queues of people in need outside his door. Sometimes he is able to use income from monasteries to fund projects, and often he will use his deacon for a practical task which might even be the repair of a church building.

62   As regards deacons in the Oriental Churches, they would appear to work in teams more than as individuals and here too there is some thought being given to the place of the diaconate. In some places the Copts, Syrians and Armenians have deaconesses, whilst the Maronites had them until the eighteenth century and are now thinking of re-establishing them.

63   Whilst the picture of the diaconate in the Orthodox and Oriental Churches suggests a somewhat static situation, there are nevertheless some people who are working for a revised diaconate of men and women.

(2) THE ROMAN CATHOLIC CHURCH

64   The restoration of a 'permanent' diaconate in the Roman Catholic Church dates formally from Vatican II, but behind *Ecclesiae Sanctae* (1966) lay some years of discussion of the issue.

65   Deacons had become significant figures in the early Church, but in the fourth century their powers were considerably curtailed and the status of the diaconate became (except in some cases) practically that of a minor order through which one had to pass before being ordained priest. At the Council of Trent (1545–63) a proposal was made that married men might receive minor orders, from deacon 'down' to doorkeeper, whilst another draft decree stated the diaconate to be so important that all churches should have a deacon as 'a helping hand of love'. However, instead of establishing a ministry of social caring, seminary training was enforced in such a way as to allow little opportunity for the exercise of minor orders and it was decided not to ordain married men.

66   It was more than three hundred years before the question was seriously raised again, and then by pastoral situations which called for a restored diaconate in many places, including South America and southern Germany. In the latter, two priests in Dachau suggested a diaconate composed of employed married men to meet the post-war home missionary situation, and their thinking was influential on Fr Joseph Hornef, whose writing on the diaconate contributed significantly to its restoration. Karl Rahner was also writing on the issue and consultations were held between Roman Catholics and members of the German Evangelical Church. From Germany there came a petition to the Catholic hierarchy throughout the world from some fifty social workers who 'wanted to try to live the diaconate in a manner that would show forth the essential functional connection between the Eucharist and the washing of feet, between the service of God and of one's brother, between the public bearing of witness through loving action and through the Gospel'.

67   When the Vatican Council agreed to the restoration of the diaconate as a permanent state not only for men vowed to celibacy but also for married men of 'more mature' years, it was left to the regional Episcopal Conferences to decide whether to proceed with the restoration of the diaconate in their territories. The decision had been made with theological and practical undergirding and outlines were

provided for selection and training. Details are left to Episcopal Conferences, but candidates are encouraged to prepare for the diaconate by spending a 'fitting time' in the revised minor orders as Lector and Acolyte, and are to receive testing and training in specially founded institutes for at least three years. In addition to being trained for teaching, 'administering the sacraments which pertain to them', visiting the sick and specifically diaconal functions, they are to be 'educated to live a truly evangelical life'. After ordination, provision is to be made for the deacon's spiritual and academic support and refreshment.

68   *Lumen Gentium,* the Dogmatic Constitution of the Church, still defines the diaconate as at the lower level of the hierarchy, and as a ministry of service. Nevertheless there is strong emphasis on liturgical duties:

> It is the duty of the deacon . . . to administer baptism solemnly, to be custodian and dispenser of the Eucharist, to assist at and bless marriages in the name of the Church, to bring Viaticum to the dying, to read the sacred Scriptures to the faithful, to instruct and exhort the people, to preside at the worship and prayers of the faithful, to administer sacramentals, and to officiate at funeral and burial services. Dedicated to the duties of charity and administration . . . (L.G. III.29).

The modern rite for the ordination of deacons in the Roman Catholic Church follows closely the words of the Constitution.

69   By the beginning of 1986 there were over 12,000 Roman Catholic 'permanent' deacons: 7500 in the USA, 1200 in Central and South America (440 of them in Brazil), 2500 in Europe (1100 in West Germany, 300 in Belgium, 260 in France) and 125 in England and Wales.

70   In the United States 79 per cent of the 144 dioceses have deacon training programmes and the length of training averages four years, although in some dioceses it lasts for five or six years. The longer-established training programmes place greater emphasis on more professional training, deeper theological teaching and more diaconal formation. In 38 dioceses the deacon candidates first undertake training for the lay ministry, which they exercise for two or three years before beginning specific diaconal formation. Increasingly, there is stress upon the communion and complementarity of ministries – lay/ diaconal, diaconal/presbyteral. Since the Church has not yet allocated much by way of financial resources for the diaconate, almost

all of the American Roman Catholic deacons are supported by salaries from their civil occupations or by a retirement pension. Apart from a very small number of celibate deacons (30–35 in religious congregations) almost all of the deacons are married.

71   The original 1971 Guidelines of the US Bishops' Committee on the Permanent Diaconate were revised in 1984 and put the ministry of love and justice before those of the Word and the liturgy. A survey in 1981 showed deacons to be serving abused children, the aged, battered women, the bereaved, the blind, the deaf, the divorced, drug addicts, the dying, the handicapped, the homeless, the sick, prisoners, refugees, the rural poor, street people and victims of racial and ethnic discrimination. Mention is also made in the Guidelines not only of the consequences but also of the root structural and institutional causes of suffering.

72   In the Roman Catholic Church in England and Wales there are five diocesan training programmes with seven dioceses taking part in them. The Archdiocese of Liverpool began with the appointment of a director for the 'permanent' diaconate in 1976 and he is supported by the diocese which, together with parishes, also pays all expenses of training and ministry. Wives are included in the selection process and share in some of the training, with a view to their being able to share in some of the deacons' non-liturgical ministry (in 1983 some 83 per cent were married men). Training consists of study for three years before, and one year after, ordination and concentrates on church history, canon law (especially that relating to marriage), inter-personal relations, liturgy, the documents of Vatican II and homiletics. More specific formation includes spiritual direction, retreat conducting and social concerns. Candidates may receive the ministry of Lector after their first year and that of Acolyte the following year. In the third year they are ordained to the diaconate, in Liverpool alongside seminarians preparing for the priesthood. Normally they are assigned to their home parishes, but there are some appointments for ministries to meet special social needs as, for example, in an urban priority area. In addition to one hour a week which candidates have with their parish priest, deacons (and their wives) meet quarterly with the Archbishop or his Auxiliary for half a day.

73   The involvement of wives in selection, training, and often ministry as well, raises the issue of women being ordained to the

diaconate in the Catholic Church. In the USA, as well as elsewhere, Roman Catholic sisters are becoming more and more involved in diaconal training and in southern Germany the question of the ordination of women to the diaconate has been proceeding along similar lines to the debate in the 1960s which preceded the establishment of a 'permanent' diaconate.

74   Inevitably the question arises in many parts of the Roman Catholic Church as to whether a married man who has been ordained to the diaconate might one day expect to be ordained to the priesthood. Added point to such a question is given by the very heavy emphasis on liturgical and quasi-priestly functions performed by deacons.

75   The threefold role of deacons, as set out by Rome, has obviously influenced the shape of their ministry: they are to serve 'in the ministry of the liturgy, of the word, and of charity'. So, to begin with, in England and Wales, 'permanent' deacons were involved primarily in parish work, and especially in taking communion to the sick and housebound and with preaching homilies. However, there are the beginnings of movement from these largely 'in house' liturgical and teaching ministries to ministries of outreach and care. Some deacons have a sense that they are ministering through their secular occupations or are developing new ministries. One man is a chiropodist and another a specialist in communications ministry; many are in demand for marriage counselling because of their being married (which, of course, the priest is not). Many would agree with the priest involved in the Clifton diocesan programme when he writes, 'we need ministers whose life is spent in the environment of every day life in our society in order to galvanise and co-ordinate on behalf of the Church the overall ministry of the Church to the world'.

76   The fact that deacons in Germany and America undertake a wide range of charitable and social ministries, whilst their counterparts in England (in both the Roman Catholic Church and the Church of England) seem to be more liturgically orientated, may suggest that cultural and social factors are at least as telling as a particular denominational understanding of the diaconate.

(3) CHURCHES OF THE REFORMATION

The Evangelical Church in Germany

77 Perhaps the most significant movement in the restoration of a social caring diaconate began in Germany in the village of Kaiserswerth near Düsseldorf. Its pastor, Theodore Fliedner, was concerned about the social conditions of the women and children in his parish and travelled to Holland and England to see what other countries were doing for disadvantaged people. In Holland he encountered deacons and deaconesses (probably Mennonites) and returned to found an organisation of women chiefly devoted to nursing (which they pioneered) and to teaching. Thus began in 1836 the Kaiserswerth Deaconesses who were commissioned by the Pastor after their training and sent, usually in twos, to work in the parishes.

78 Originally all the candidates undertook to remain in the institute for five years, but this soon became a life commitment for the single or widowed women. Numerous charitable institutions have been supplied by them with workers, not only in Germany but also in Jerusalem, Alexandria, Cairo and other places where German culture has spread. They are still strong in West Germany and their influence contributed to the recovery of the Order of Deaconesses in the Church of England.

79 Three years before the Kaiserswerth foundation a pastor in Hamburg, Johannes Wichern, founded the Rauhes Haus in order to provide for the material and spiritual needs of poor children through family education. A number of houses became training centres for helpers and some of them formed themselves into a Deacon Brotherhood. Another deacon brotherhood grew out of Wichern's *Johannisstift*, which he founded for the purpose of prison reform, and during the wars of 1864, 1866 and 1870 he and the brothers organised the *Felddiakonie* for helping the wounded.

80 At about the same period some twenty further deacon brotherhoods came into being, the best known of which is the present *Westfälische Diakonieanstalt Nazareth* in Bethel, which consists of both men and women, the latter having been admitted in the 1950s. At first these brotherhoods belonged to voluntary 'Inner Mission' associations, in spite of Wichern's plea to the Church in 1848 that it should be responsible for them. So the brotherhood provided training, commissioning and work in institution, hospital or parish, and

arranged facilities for retirement, in-service training, conferences or holidays. It took Hitler's ban on voluntary associations for the Church to take them into its care and from then on the brotherhoods were rooted in its structure, and their members now received their blessing or commissioning from the Church rather than from the brotherhood.

81   Sadly, a few brotherhoods were 'legally' split when Germany was partitioned, but in spite of a drop in numbers after two World Wars, the number of deacons has risen from 3566 in 1915 to 6074 in 1982. There are some 16 West German brotherhoods, totalling in 1986 some 7303 members, of which 3925 are active; the largest brotherhood has 1103 members. There are about 1000 deacons in seven East German brotherhoods.

82   The Church states in its 1948 Constitution: 'The diaconate is an expression of church existence, a task of church life . . . There must be leadership in diaconally motivated social action.' Of those who become deacons there are three requirements:

that they be consecrated by the Church (this is not to be understood in the same way as ordination into the single ministry which belongs to the pastor);

that they be qualified not only through a theological course approved and examined by the Church, but also through a government-approved social service course;

that they belong to a brotherhood or diaconal fellowship and live in the brotherhood during their training, so as to learn to build community. (They are not under religious vows and most deacons are married.)

83   Their government-approved training is in various forms of social work, such as being a housefather or warden, nursing, psychiatric care, youth work, religious education and teaching. Some 48 per cent of deacons in 1982 were in institutional work (including one in charge of a hospital radio station and another responsible for public relations for a hospital), with 2 per cent in government posts, 19 per cent in district (supervisory) work and 26 per cent in parish work, equivalent to that undertaken by an Anglican Accredited Lay Worker, with or without youth or community work; less than 1 per cent are used for the administration of brotherhoods.

84   Deacons are now trained to give short homilies and conduct 'assembly' type religious services, especially for their own residential

units or in the smaller institutions. Larger institutions would have pastors as chaplains. The deacons' influence contributed to the restoration of the distinctive diaconate by the Roman Catholic Church, which ordained its first distinctive deacon in Cologne Cathedral in 1968.

85 Those deaconesses who have grown up out of the Kaiserswerth model are unmarried and usually live in communal groups under the care of a mother-house which is linked to Kaiserswerth. Formerly there was community of goods, with the deaconesses receiving only pocket-money, but recent changes in hospital finance have meant that in some cases the deaconesses draw a salary.

86 There are also other associations of Diaconal Sisters, providing initial and in-service training in nursing, as well as pastoral and professional support and facilities for holidays and retirement. Many of the sisters are salaried district nurses living independently who relate more to their parish church than to a hospital or training house chapel. Although it is expected that pastoral work will be left to the pastor, the sisters obviously have many pastoral and evangelistic opportunities in their nursing work. The 'third order' members of Kaiserswerth, once termed 'Associate Sisters' and now known also as diaconal sisters, may include men and married women: one of these groups is experimenting with a five-year commitment. The number of sisters in both East and West Germany who are still active is somewhere between 10,000 and 11,000, spread between six major German associations of deaconesses and diaconal sisters. This represents about 60 per cent of the world total of women of all denominations in full-time diaconal ministry.

87 The various associations, sisterhoods and brotherhoods have come about not simply because of the process of history but because the deaconesses and deacons have themselves required pastoral support and opportunities for in-service training, as well as peer-group encouragement whilst undertaking diaconal work. Diaconal associations also ensure that the churches give both support and recognition to the brothers and sisters.

88 Thus each of the constituent Churches of the Evangelical Church has a major department devoted to diaconal work. The many diaconal institutions usually have a pastor who is appointed not only to care for the staff (patients or other recipients of care might have, in

addition, their own pastor), but also to act as business manager and to liaise with outside organisations employing nurses from their institution. It is these pastors, rather than the deacons and deaconesses themselves, who are chiefly involved with the theology of the diaconate.

Other Lutheran Churches

89   In those Scandinavian countries where the Lutheran Church is strong, there is a variety of deacon brotherhoods and deaconess sisterhoods. Some are similar to the pattern of the German Evangelical Church, whilst many are linked primarily and closely with their parish churches.

90   In the Church of Sweden there is no transitional diaconate but men and women alike are ordained by the bishop to a life-long distinctive diaconate, exercised either in a parish for pastoral work or in a variety of tasks within the community. They may be given permission by the bishop to preach and to administer the Holy Communion. Their training combines both theology and professional skills (from social work to church music) within the context of a brotherhood or sisterhood, and the mother houses play an important role in training and support. In 1983 there were some 4040 women in full-time diaconal ministry in Finland and Scandinavia, as well as some 600 men.

91   Since 1945 representatives of the associations of women involved in *diakonia* have met every four years in the Diakonia Assembly, whilst the European Conference of Deacons was established in 1969 to exchange information and fellowship among the various Protestant associations of deacons in East and West Germany, Denmark, Finland, France, the Netherlands, Norway, Sweden and Switzerland. 'Koinonia-Diakonia' is a working party composed of people from these two organisations, with the addition of Catholics from their International Diaconate Centre, Orthodox and WCC staff, which is attempting to work on theological questions concerning the diaconate. It has also held two conferences (L'Abresle, 1976, and Coventry, 1983).

92   In America, Lutheran deacons and deaconesses have developed locally and are said to have no official status in their Churches, belonging rather to voluntary agencies. Nevertheless, the *Deaconess*

Community of the Lutheran Church in America (in Gladwyn, Pennsylvania) is affirmed by and under the direction of that Church.

93   The Lutheran Church in America, however, is in process of uniting with the American Lutheran Church and with the Association of Evangelical Lutheran Churches to form (as from January 1988) the Evangelical Lutheran Church in America. Among the provisions of the merger is that 'those persons named as deacons or deaconesses in the uniting churches will be received into the ELCA with that status, pending the outcome of a six-year study of ministry, to be completed in 1994.'[11]

94   The Missouri Synod is not party to this scheme and is among those Lutheran Churches which makes use of the men's *Order of St Stephen* in Baltimore, some of whose members are set apart as part-time liturgical assistants. The Missouri Synod in 1967 made a sharp differentiation between deacons and clergy, noting them to be 'elected (male) officers of the congregation'. In 1981, however, a document speaks of 'ordination' to 'public ministry' (for which women are not eligible), 'commissioning' to an 'office auxiliary to pastoral ministry', and 'installation' into a specific post or auxiliary office.

95   Deaconesses are commissioned and the Missouri Synod Lutheran Deaconess Association had until 1987 a Deaconess House and an administrator at Valparaiso University. The house has now been disposed of and has been replaced by the *Center for Diaconal Ministry* as an administrative office, with the women being placed in university accommodation. The Missouri Synod provides (at Valparaiso University, USA) a four-year training for diaconal ministers who are commissioned after a year's internship and are classified as lay workers.

The Reformed Churches

96   In the Reformed tradition ordination is reserved for the ministers of word and sacrament, whilst deacons and deaconesses are elected or appointed, sometimes for a set period of time. In origin, they were officers of the congregation, responsible for collecting the alms of the believers and distributing them to those in need. This was how Calvin saw and used them, and in the Dutch Reformed tradition there are three orders: life-long ministers of word and sacrament, elders and deacons who are appointed for a period. The diaconal office receives

liturgical expression in the taking up of the collection and in the distribution of Holy Communion. Every congregation has deacons as well as elders, all of them being perceived as lay officers. In the USA the Christian Reformed Church reflects the same practice.

97 Some disciplinary responsibilities have on occasion been expected of them, as, for example, among the Pilgrim Fathers when deacons were used to wake up those who fell asleep during the sermon. The Mennonite deaconesses in nineteenth century Holland impressed Pastor Fliedner of Kaiserswerth with their social care, as did the Dutch Reformed deacons whose numbers were matched to the size of the congregation. Eventually the Dutch deaconesses became totally involved in hospitals and were separated from their parish base, which perhaps accounts in part for their diminishing numbers since World War II.

98 At the beginning of 1987 the Dutch deaconesses, deacons and diaconal workers united into the *Association of Diaconal Workers*, which numbers some 400 members. They are professional people working in churches, hospitals, schools and social work, and those who wish to join the Association (having been professionally trained) must attend Bible study. Membership involves mutual support and the opportunity of discussion of their diaconal ministries.

99 In 1974 Robert W. Henderson wrote *Profile of the Eldership* for the World Alliance of Reformed Churches, in which he sees the elder as a deacon who specialises in spiritual matters. With modest theological education, the elder has but rarely any public, liturgical or preaching functions, but a wide pastoral and spiritual role, with the care of the sick, poor and oppressed, which he exercises perhaps with others who may be termed 'deacons'. He has a strong role in local church government, and the congregation usually has a strong voice in the selection for eldership which is (at least theoretically held for a set time. In only one church – Christian Church (Disciples) USA – would an elder preside at the Lord's table. Henderson recommended that the traditional eldership be remodelled under the rubrics for an amplified diaconate, with an ordination parallel to that of presbyters.

100 In Canada the former deaconesses of the United Church in Canada are now included as Diaconal Ministers of the United Church of Canada, who number some 232 (both male and female, active and retired). The Presbyterian Church in Canada includes female

missionaries (who used to be termed deaconesses) in its Order of Diaconal Ministries.

101   In the Church of Scotland, in addition to congregational elders, there were in 1986 some 60 deaconesses. Of these, 37 were employed by congregations for work among parishioners and 18 were employed in other diaconal ministries, especially as hospital chaplains. Some are now pioneering new diaconal projects which reach out further into the local community. Policy, selection and training are in the hands of the Diaconate Board, and a two-year programme of training leads to the Certificate of Studies in Diaconal Ministry at St Colm's College. Commissioning follows in a service by presbytery and only those with full (university) theological training are allowed to preach. There are as yet no male deacons, although the diaconate was opened up to men in 1981. Largely for financial and pastoral reasons, trained men are more apt to be employed as Lay Agents.

102   In the Presbyterian Church of Ireland there are about 25 deaconesses. They are trained at St Colm's College with their Scottish counterparts and finance for this, as also for their work, comes from groups of church women. One aspect of their work has been to pioneer 'Friendship Houses'.

The Methodist Churches

103   In Britain, diaconal and pastoral activities have always been shared in large measure by the ordained ministry and the laity. In these, 'Class Leaders' and 'Communion Stewards' have played a large part.

104   The Wesley Deaconess Order, a Lay Order founded in 1890 on the model of Pastor Fliedner's work in Germany, is designed to be a fellowship of mutual care for others, under the vow of obedience and with a commitment to evangelism in the widest sense. The Order was at first occupied in social and pastoral work among women, but for many years now most Deaconesses have also been Local Preachers; many have been placed in pastoral charge of Methodist Churches (often with a 'dispensation', a special limited authorisation, to preside at Holy Communion). In recent years some Deaconesses have been engaged in social and education work outside the Church.

Deaconesses are 'ordained' (in an unusual sense), and recognised by the Conference. Until 1967, but not since then, they have resigned on marriage.

105   As soon as women could be ordained to the ministry of Word and Sacrament (in 1974), many Deaconesses became ordained ministers and the Order's size was greatly reduced. Recruitment was suspended in 1977 but has been resumed, and the Order is now open to men (though a new name is not yet determined). In 1987, the first year after new recruitment and the first year in which men were eligible, eight women and four men were accepted by the Conference. A call received from God and confirmed by the Church, and a willingness to be part of a supportive system of training, discipline, obedience and accountability, are the required qualifications. No precise academic credentials are required nor the wish to preach.

106   It should be decided in 1988 whether the Church will set up a 'Methodist Order for Mission and Ministry' (MOMM), open to paid and unpaid Church Workers in certain offices. If it is set up, it is proposed that members of the Wesley Deaconess Order (under its new name) would be eligible for it, but this proposal is by no means certain to be adopted.

107   In the United Methodist Church of the USA, men and women who are to be ordained as 'elders' (i.e. ministers) are first ordained as deacons, and serve as such normally for two years. Distinct from the deacons are those in the recently established office of 'diaconal ministers'; these men and women accept a lifelong vocation, and are authorised by an 'act of consecration'. They are not called deacons. Their 'called out' and 'set apart' ministry is church-related, and their functions may be pastoral, charitable, liturgical, educational or administrative, or more than one of these. They are to exemplify the servanthood of all Christians.

108   The Methodist Church in New Zealand has, since 1976, formally recognised presbyters and deacons as belonging to separate orders of ministry, each with a distinctive vocation and task in the Church's mission. 'Deacons are engaged in ministries which are *examples* to the whole Church of its *servant* ministry, usually on the cutting-edge of the Church's life.'[12] These deacons are ordained for life by prayer and the laying-on of hands and are mostly self-supporting, with some employed in full-time church work. This diaconate is seen

as a life-long ordained ministry of service which takes many forms but is directed towards the community. It is not necessary for a deacon to have any liturgical functions, although there should always be 'some links with congregational life and activity'.

3 The Diaconate in the Anglican Communion[13]

(1) THE EPISCOPAL CHURCH OF THE UNITED STATES OF AMERICA

109 In ECUSA – which, with about three million Church members (Baptised Persons),[14] is roughly the same size as the Church of England – there were at the end of 1986 nearly 900 'vocational' deacons, with a further 350 in training and some 300 aspirants. Most of these are married, and more than 40 per cent of them are women. Their ministry is mostly non-stipendiary and 'part-time' (10–15 hours a week given to specifically church work) and there are about as many 'vocational' deacons as there are non-stipendiary priests.

110 This is in marked contrast to a situation whereby the diaconate developed a negative image in the 1940s and 1950s, when some men were ordained to be 'perpetual deacons'. They were usually noted for their faithfulness to the parish priest and had a ministry almost always limited to the sanctuary, usually as administrators of the chalice.

111 The present situation takes its origins partly from the liturgical movement 'Associated Parishes' in the early 1970s and partly from the National Center for the Diaconate (NCD), which between 1974 and 1985 worked to promote a 'permanent' diaconate. This was partly financed by the Trustees of the former Central House for Deaconesses, after its approximately fifty deaconesses were declared by ECUSA in 1970 to be in the diaconate.

112 In 1986 the NCD was reconstituted to include Canadians as the North American Association for the Diaconate (NAAD), with membership open to dioceses, organisations and individuals. It works closely with an official ECUSA body, the Commission for the Development of Ministry (CDM), which is commonly seen to be concerned to 'protect' the ministry of the laity, and which has contributed several helpful reports on diaconal ministry.

113 Most dioceses have a Commission for Ministry (often with a

diaconate sub-committee) and in nearly two-thirds of them there are programmes for diaconate development. Selection (as with the priesthood) is undertaken by each diocese with procedures which are similar but not identical. In some of them, particularly in the beginning, the first stage is for priests to nominate for selection people already exercising a diaconal ministry. A new development in one diocese (Pittsburgh) requires the candidate to participate before the normal selection process in a year-long programme which includes nine months of supervised field experience, ministering as a lay person.

114 A large proportion of the applicants in ECUSA are college graduates, although the emphasis is on a serving ministry which responds to pastoral needs. Certainly this was the vision of James Lowery, head of NCD, who wrote in 1980, 'ordained Deacons personify, sacramentalize, and enable that ministry of service to which all Christians are called at baptism'. It is generally accepted that social serving ministries need to be emphasised more than liturgical ministries, although deacons should exercise both.

115 As with selection, the diocese is also responsible for training. There is no ECUSA ministerial training scheme, and whilst candidates for the priesthood attend residential seminary, those for the diaconate are trained non-residentially. Classes occur in the evenings and at weekends, using parochial clergy and diocesan buildings. The director of the programme is usually on the diocesan staff but other costs are only partly met by the diocese, with the students meeting the rest (sometimes helped by their parishes).

116 Most dioceses have a special three-year training programme for deacons which includes theological subjects, pastoral experience and spiritual formation. Some make use of the Education for Ministry course, some use seminary-model training, whilst some provide a course which includes not only deacon candidates but also interested laity, with a couple of extra courses for the deacons. Pittsburgh, with its rich facilities, is able to devise individual training programmes.

117 Some of the bishops have a clear concept of deacons as being diocesan-based so that they can reach out into the world and be sent, either individually or in a team, into any area of need or special emergency. In one diocese (Nevada) a deacon who has a theological degree has been entrusted by the bishop to run a diocesan programme

to enable each Church member to 'realise the opportunity to serve Christ in the Church and world'. Deacons in Hawaii, California and other dioceses are being trained to enable the laity in their ministries. Where there is diocesan-based diaconal ministry it may include the following: social service on behalf of the diocese; training of new deacons; diocesan education; administration for regional councils of churches; suicide prevention programmes (especially in jails); prison chaplaincy; ministry to the deaf; scouting (especially training of leaders); co-ordination of ministries to colleges; hospital and hospice chaplaincy; healing ministry; cathedral administration and ministry to the cathedral congregation.

118   The great majority of deacons are based in parishes and almost all of them are non-stipendiary, although the parish pays their expenses. Dioceses differ in their policy as to whether the deacon serves in the home parish, or whether she or he is deployable in a neighbouring parish. Included within the ministry of parochially-based deacons are: co-ordination of visiting in hospitals and nursing homes by laity, priests and deacons; organisation of educational programmes for adults, Sunday schools and special events; youth work; outreach to the community through links with the social services, advising people on completion of official forms, finding and using volunteers and professional staff, and linking with fraternal or voluntary organisations such as Lions, Rotary, etc.; instructing laity involved in public worship, such as readers (who in ECUSA are not licensed to preach), ushers, acolytes and the new Lay Eucharistic Ministers.

119   A sample letter of Agreement for Parish Deacons (recommended by NAAD) states:

> All ministries of the parish are exercised under the oversight of the bishop of the diocese and under the immediate leadership and authority of the pastor and vestry.
>
> The fundamental ministry of the deacon is to hold before the Church the character of the whole ministry of the Church as service and of her ministers as servants.

120   Most deacons have liturgical functions in the parishes in which they work and the new American BCP makes rubrical provision for these. In addition to the customary parts of the Eucharist and the administration of the Reserved Sacrament to the housebound, the

deacon may anoint the sick and may assist in baptisms, weddings and funerals.

121　Eucharistic preaching is not automatically part of the deacon's liturgical duties, but may be authorised by the bishop. However, the sample Letter of Agreement says 'the pastor is the ordinary preacher of the parish. In services conducted by the deacon, the deacon is the ordinary preacher.' It goes on to say:

> In liturgical service at . . . Church, the deacon shall not function in roles proper to priests or other persons, and priests or other persons in the parish shall not exercise liturgical functions proper to the deacons or wear vestments suggestive of the diaconate.

122　Whilst in ECUSA there is no equivalent to a rural deanery, a number of parishes sometimes come together for a particular project. So some deacons in the diocese of California have joined forces for the training of the laity from their area for specific ministries to hospitals and jails. Funding for this may come either from local parishes, 'Episcopal Charities' or similar sources, or the deacons concerned may join or form charitable agencies for their own support when the ministry demands all their time. Other such joint enterprises include city mission work and a ministry to those over 60 by deacons working with other agencies.

123　Thus there is great variety in the types, bases, forms of support and life-styles of the deacons. Many are involved in social caring work in the local community, rather than exclusively in the parish, and some who are employed by caring agencies exercise their ministry mainly through their civil profession. Some deacons, mostly women, are full-time, salaried and employed by special agencies (perhaps formed by themselves, such as a resource centre for women widowed or divorced). They might contract with parishes or others for the deployment of their skills. In one diocese (Hawaii) are a ministry to non-responsive patients in hospital, and a ministry to tourists who are stranded (perhaps through illness). At least one parish has a deacon as a parish administrator, who ranks as an 'associate to the rector'. A few deacons are in charge of missions, where the congregations are too small or too poor to be parishes. It is not unusual for the deacon to 'preside' at the Eucharist in a mission (or even in a parish), using the Reserved Sacrament, though the sample Letter of Agreement does not encourage this.

124   It is evident that diaconate programmes are expanding in ECUSA and the concept of 'vocational' deacons is being accepted by laity and clergy alike. With the development by NAAD of training resources for use by dioceses, it is possible that there will be less variation between dioceses in selection, training and deployment of deacons.

125   The sample Letter of Agreement forbids 'special dress, titles, perquisites and other symbols of a clerical status which distinguish the deacon sharply from those among whom the deacon lives and works and whom the deacon serves', although clerical wear is permitted for liturgical occasions and pastoral visits to institutions. The title 'Deacon' is encouraged.

126   It would seem that the 'vocational' diaconate in America has developed a leadership for service and thereby has both alerted the Church to its responsibility to society and also enabled new ministries of outreach by laity as well as deacons. There is increasing emphasis on deacons identifying needs and responding with appropriate ministries.

(2) THE CHURCH OF THE PROVINCE OF SOUTHERN AFRICA[15]

127   The move towards the reform of the diaconate in the CPSA began in the late 1970s, with consideration by the Provincial Synod of the matter, leading to the appointment of a commission. This reported in 1981 and its recommendations to 'restore' the diaconate were accepted by the Province. Their acceptance involves both the ordination of women to the diaconate and the amendment of those rubrics and canons which create the impression of the diaconate's being but a stepping-stone to the priesthood.

128   It seems to have been left largely to the eighteen dioceses to take up the recommendations, and their implementation has been patchy and slow. The diocese of Johannesburg, with three already ordained and a further six (including one woman) training for ordination, probably has the most people, but in the Province as a whole between 10 and 15 women had been ordained to the distinctive diaconate by Trinity Sunday 1987.

129   Selection of candidates for the diaconate (as for the priesthood) is by dioceses, using procedures based on ACCM's selection

conference. Usually there are both priest and deacon candidates at the same conference, although a distinction is made with respect to qualifications and criteria.

130   Training, too, is primarily under diocesan auspices, and some unofficial guidelines were suggested in 1982 by the Reverend Stephen Hayes of Pretoria (who took the lead in convincing the Church that it should take the diaconate seriously). He suggests that at least part of the training should be undertaken with priest-candidates, both because priest-candidates spend some time in the diaconate, and because priests may well be working in a team which includes deacons.

131   It is accepted that the training should be broad enough to incorporate many different forms of the diaconate. A uniform syllabus was not thought to be appropriate, although there might be a common core of biblical, theological and liturgical subjects. Thereafter the deacon candidate would be trained in economics, administration, welfare or development, as appropriate to the individual's needs and circumstances and as the diocese determined. Any training scheme should take account of the flexibility of the diaconate and its variety of ministries.

132   For deacon candidates with suitable educational qualifications there is under consideration by the University of South Africa (which operates by correspondence courses as well as lectures and seminars) a degree course for the degree of B.Diac. This consists of five groups of subjects: theology, administration, development, social work and general (languages, communications and law).

133   There is little information to hand of the way the few distinctive deacons are being used in the CPSA. They are almost all non-stipendiary and parochial thus far. From being called 'permanent' deacons at first they are now commonly referred to as 'distinctive' deacons.

134   Of interest is the thinking which has led to the restoration of the diaconate. Whilst much of it has direct application to the Church elsewhere, it clearly reflects the situation in South Africa. The main reason for setting up the commission was the recognition by a Partners-in-Mission Consultation that the Church had to do more to meet the needs of the poor and oppressed in an *apartheid* society.

135   Stress is placed on diaconal ministry being seen within the total ministry of the Church:

> There is little point in restoring one ministry in the Church when most of the other ministries remain dormant. Thus a restoration of the diaconate should be seen as one aspect of a total renewal of the Church as the Body of Christ.

136   A tendency is noted in the life of the Church towards a cleavage between social action and evangelism, with people opting for one or other side, whereas the diaconal model of the Seven in Acts 6 shows the inter-relationship of service and proclamation, since at least two of the Seven were active evangelists as well. A restoration of the diaconate would recognise social concern as a proper part of the Church's ministry.

137   In no way need this detract from the ministry of the laity, for God will always raise up men and women for a ministry of service to the poor and oppressed who will not necessarily be called to ordained ministry. 'However, having deacons who are set apart to order and encourage such work would greatly help those who are already involved in it, as well as making it apparent to those who see such ministry as "unspiritual" that it is an integral and recognised part of the ministry of the Church as the Body of Christ.'

138   With regard to diaconal ministry within the Church, there are situations, particularly within rural parishes, where a deacon would be in a much better position than the hard-pressed priest (with maybe as many as twenty congregations in his care) to relieve the 'sick, poor and impotent people of the parish'. All too often, continuing dependency on 'outside' relief is increased by the distribution of aid from outside the parish; often the priest does not know those to whom he is distributing relief, with the result that there are many 'widows' who are neglected in the distribution.

139   Instead, a deacon would seek aid, first among the parishioners and only afterwards from outside the parish, so that 'dependency is not increased, but rather the members of the Body are encouraged to care for each other, and so the Body builds itself up in love'. But

> This kind of ministry does not just happen. It needs the power of the Spirit moving among people to persuade them of their need for Christ, to build them into a community which cares for its members, and then that caring needs to be developed, ordered and channelled along the lines suggested in

Acts 6. If it is to be effective, the priests cannot do it, without neglecting their own distinctive ministry. It needs men (*sic*) full of the Holy Spirit and wisdom, specially set aside for that task of *diakonia*.

140   The restoration of the diaconate is justified not as a temporary expedient, to cope with the particular social needs of present-day South Africa, but as essential to the life of the Church. Gal. 6.10 suggests 'doing good' to *all*, in addition to 'our brothers in the faith', and at a very early stage Christian care was extended to the pagan poor as well as to those within the Christian fellowship. 'The last pagan Roman emperor, Julian the Apostate, could complain that "the godless Galileans feed not only their own (poor) but ours also".'

141   Consideration needs to be given to biblical teaching on poverty and wealth, and to the responsibility of Christians as stewards with their need to exercise political and economic power not for their own sake but for the sake of giving service. Such service to the world, as the ministry of Christ, belongs to the whole Church and there is 'far more scriptural authority for speaking of a *diakonia* of all believers than there is for speaking for (*sic*) a priesthood (presbyterate) of all believers'. So, whilst it is the task of deacons to order and encourage the ministry of *diakonia,* it is exercised by the whole Body.

142   Among particular opportunities of service the whole area of investment is important. The use and administration of church funds, as well as the morality of the financial policies of large commercial organisations, point to the need to have deacons 'trained in economics, accountancy and similar disciplines, as well as in theology'. It may be right to question the investment of funds 'as worldly wisdom dictates, and not as guided by the Spirit of God'. After all, deacons in the early Church often performed the work now done by church treasurers.

143   Another traditional area of diaconal ministry has been in orphanages, hospitals, clinics, development agencies and other institutions. These could appropriately be staffed by deacons, because 'to be a warden of an orphanage or a church hospital requires more than worldly wisdom or a degree in administration or social work. It requires the grace of the Holy Spirit, in order that it may be seen that this is the diaconal work of the Church'.

144   Although the State has taken over much of the Church's former welfare work, there is still a place for diaconal ministry and 'the poor

are still with us'. Ascertaining people's rights and 'helping people to overcome bureaucratic obstacles, as well as fraud and corruption, is a diaconal ministry which is very much needed'.

145   In the CPSA it would seem that whilst a good deal of thinking has been done concerning the distinctive diaconate, it has still to be tested in practice.

(3) THE SCOTTISH EPISCOPAL CHURCH[16]

146   The Scottish Episcopal Church was one of the earliest Churches of the Anglican Communion to approve the re-establishment of a 'permanent' diaconate, on the basis of the Report of the Committee on the Diaconate in 1965. But although the possibility of a 'permanent' diaconate has been open to men for some twenty years, few have availed themselves of it and the majority of those who offered initially for the ministry have subsequently become priests. It may be that in spite of emphasis being placed on the caring role of deacons in the community, they are still widely regarded as being primarily liturgical ministers. Both the 1929 and 1984 liturgies of the SEC describe their functions in practical, as well as liturgical terms.

147   However, it is possible that, with the opening of the diaconate in the SEC to women, there may be more enthusiasm among men for this ministry. The decision to admit women to the Order was agreed by the General Synod in June 1986, a previous attempt in November 1981 having failed to gain the necessary majority in the First Chamber. Previously there had been deaconesses in the SEC, appointed with prayer and the laying-on of hands, often by the same form of service as deacons. Canonically they were not in Holy Orders, voted with the laity, and were listed in the Year Book under Lay Ministries. In practice they performed many of the traditional duties of deacons, including assisting at the Eucharist and pastoral work. The order of deaconesses still exists, although almost all of its members have now been ordained deacon and are now in Holy Orders.

148   Since June 1986 the diaconate has consisted of men and women. Most male deacons expect later to be ordained priest, but a few men and all the women form a 'permanent' diaconate. Many are non-stipendiary, but in the middle of 1987 there were five deacons

functioning full-time in the church, all of them women, and two of them were in the traditional parish ministry.

149   Functions vary, but they are mostly liturgical, sacramental and pastoral, although they may be involved in the wider community. Their work is designated either by the bishop or by their rector and they are given a particular appointment by licence from the bishop.

150   It should be noted that among kindred ministries there are both Lay Readers (women as well as men) and Women Workers. The former are involved in conducting worship and preaching and often have other leadership roles in the congregation. Their licence is either diocesan or congregational and does not necessarily demand a lifetime commitment. Women Workers are licensed by the bishop for a particular piece of pastoral work, either in a parish or in the wider community in the area of social responsibility. Theirs is a stipendiary appointment and may be either full- or part-time.

151   A paper from the Doctrine Committee of the Scottish Episcopal Church, in preparation for the debate in 1986 concerning the admission of women to the diaconate, seeks to provide background and to set out the arguments 'on both sides'. Whilst it does not argue a case for or against a 'permanent' diaconate, it points out that the arguments both for and against contain speculative elements, 'e.g. on potential renewal; on possible numbers offering; on the pastoral and ecumenical effects'. It goes on to say:

> The revival of a permanent diaconate need not lead to the loss or detriment of lay ministries, provided goodwill and commonsense are exercised – though it could do so. It need not lead to a clericalization of the laity, particularly if there is flexibility over such matters as clerical dress, use of titles like 'The Reverend', etc. – but it could do so. It may not lead to ecumenical progress – but it might do so. The ecumenical situation demands that we do something about our diaconate; many would be reluctant to abolish it; many see the situation as unsatisfactory left as it is. The possibility of a distinctive diaconate of men and women at least deserves serious consideration: we cannot tell how many might be called to it unless we try it. Many of those who long for the presence of women in the presbyterate would positively welcome their presence in the diaconate. Those who cannot agree to the ordination of women as priests need not see this as 'the thin end of the wedge', when the ordination would be to a permanent or distinctive diaconate.

(4) SOME OTHER PROVINCES AND DIOCESES

Australia

152 Dioceses differ in their practice, but in the diocese of Melbourne steps are being taken to formalise the selection, training and ordination of men and women for the distinctive diaconate. Most of those who are already 'permanent' deacons are either the few men who for some personal or disciplinary reason have not been ordained priest or those women who have been ordained to the diaconate until such time as the priesthood is open to them.

153 A Report by the Diocesan Committee on the Diaconate (1987) emphasises the deacon's being 'publicly responsible for the Gospel' and sees her or his ministry as being exercised in education, welfare, administration, healing ministry and pastoral work. For many of those in the caring professions there is a continuity in their ministry, both before and after ordination, but 'ordination means being placed to some degree at the church's disposal'.

154 Selection and training are thoroughly and carefully detailed and those selected are initially 'candidates in training', being described as 'ordinands' about a year before ordination.

Ireland

155 There is no distinctive diaconate in the Church of Ireland, but as in many other places there is a permanent diaconate for those women who await the possibility of ordination to the priesthood. The first woman deacon was ordained in June 1987, to be parochially-based and stipendiary. There are three others in training, one of them at Trinity College, Dublin, for a three-year course, the other two being trained for non-stipendiary ministry by means of a three-year part-time course which is mainly diocesan-based. Men and women candidates for ordination train together.

New Zealand

156 The question of a distinctive diaconate is likely to be considered by the General Synod in 1988, in preparation for which a report is being discussed by dioceses. As both the priesthood and the diaconate are open to both sexes, those who remain as deacons are the few who, after ordination to the diaconate, have not proceeded to the

priesthood; their reasons have generally been personal rather than vocational.

South America

157 Distances make for difficulty in communication, but the issue of the diaconate is certainly around. It is generally agreed both that the use of the diaconate simply as a stepping-stone to the priesthood is unsatisfactory and that there is a need to develop the proper exercise of diaconal functions in and by the Body of Christ. Questions are being asked as to whether the chief functions of the deacon are liturgical or pastoral (without responsibilities for leadership) or administrative. A common fear is that the church could become unduly clericalised by emphasising a permanent *order* of deacons.

158 Impressions suggest that there may be one or two distinctive deacons in Peru, and perhaps one in Southern Argentina. The Canons of the Diocese of Chile provide for such deacons but have not thus far been invoked because of a lack of full understanding of the role of the distinctive deacon.

Wales

159 No decision has been taken to set up a permanent Order of Deacons. However, in 1979 the Governing Body took the decision to ordain women deacons. Consequently at the end of 1986 there were 22 women deacons, of whom 17 are stipendiary and 5 are non-stipendiary; at the same time there were 34 male deacons (29 stipendiary, 5 NSM), all of whom expect to be ordained to the priesthood. The training for all ordained ministry is the same: an appropriate time at theological college for stipendiary ministry and a diocesan part-time scheme for the non-stipendiary. All are licensed to parishes.

160 Some (though probably very few) of the women deacons see their vocation as being to the diaconate, but most of them feel called to the priestly ministry and find their position as 'permanent' deacons increasingly irritating.

4   Diaconal Ministries in the Church of England Today

(1) INTRODUCTION

161   The picture of diaconal ministry in the Church of England is not a tidy one, nor is it uniform across the dioceses. It is confused by a variety of categories used to describe the forms of diaconal ministry: lay and ordained; professional and non-professional; stipendiary and non-stipendiary; local/diocesan and national; full-time and part-time; permanent deacons and distinctive deacons; as well as a variety of terminology to describe pastoral lay ministers. The description in what follows is based upon answers to a questionnaire (see Appendix 2) sent to every diocesan and area bishop in February 1987. The response to the questionnaire was very high and 48 dioceses (or episcopal areas) returned questionnaires relating to at least some of the categories.

162   The questions related to six spheres of non-episcopal and non-priestly ministry: accredited lay workers, deaconesses, the Church Army, readers, distinctive deacons, and pastoral lay ministers. Information in each sphere was sought concerning the numbers involved, selection, training, licensing and the tasks of ministry being carried out. A final question, much more difficult both to answer and to summarise, asked for information about how the role of that particular sphere of ministry was perceived. Nearly all the replies to this spoke of functions rather than the nature of the ministry.

163   There is no significance attached to the order in which the various 'diaconal' ministries have been placed and what follows is a generalised and impressionistic picture, based upon the answers to the questions. (Detailed statistical information is included in Appendix 3 to this Report and in Appendix 5 there is a note on the present situation with regard to Church Social Workers.) There is always, of course, the danger that an attempt to summarise what is a complex and untidy scene will not do full justice to the many

dynamic, flexible and spontaneous patterns of diaconal ministry that undoubtedly exist.

(2) ACCREDITED LAY WORKERS

164   Forty-two dioceses employ 154 Accredited Lay Workers (both men and women). These may be either stipendiary or non-stipendiary, full-time or part-time. There are significantly more women amongst this group and only 23 men. Seventeen dioceses employ stipendiary males and three dioceses employ local non-stipendiary workers. Fourteen of the 17 dioceses have only one stipendiary male. Lincoln has three and London/Willesden and Chichester have two each. This compares with 28 dioceses which employ stipendiary women, although no dioceses has more than five. Of the 29 dioceses that employ non-stipendiary women, none has more than six.

165   Selection in almost all cases is done through a national selection process, apart from a few dioceses where there is a selection process within the diocese itself. In only one diocese is selection done by the Bishop. The normal pattern for training is at a theological college or by a recognised non-residential ministerial training scheme. In a few cases courses are devised by the diocese (Chichester, Truro, Canterbury and Worcester) and in one instance a national youth course has been used. The length of training varies from two to four years, three years being the most common. The main source of funding is central church funds, with some help coming from the Church Pastoral Aid Society, LEA grants, or parochial contributions. Licences in the majority of cases are for work in the parish or the diocese, and only infrequently to a deanery post. In special cases Accredited Lay Workers are licensed to work in a hospital, a diocesan conference centre, a counselling centre, an industrial mission, to oversee some special area of social work or to act as a diocesan lay ministry adviser. In the majority of dioceses the licences are for an indefinite period. Bradford has five-year contracts, similar to those for team vicars. In the case of a special piece of work, the licence may be for a limited period (e.g. hospital chaplaincies, local ecumenical projects or team or sector ministries). In Portsmouth a licence is granted for three years in the first instance and is then renewable every five years.

166   In addition to general parochial ministry, the tasks carried out by Accredited Lay Workers are indistinguishable from those of a deacon/deaconess, with the exception of the permission given to the deacon to conduct marriages and (in the absence of the priest) to baptise. A number of them are given identifiable specialist tasks within the parochial ministry: pre- and post-baptismal care, care of the bereaved, ministry to the sick, counselling, teaching, preaching, liturgical duties, work with children and young people and outreach.

167   Some Accredited Lay Workers are employed for particular forms of specialised ministry outside the parish. In three dioceses the Diocesan Lay Ministry Adviser is an Accredited Lay Worker. Other specialist posts include a diocesan development and training officer, a diocesan missioner, a parish youth worker, a theological college teacher, a chaplain to the deaf, the warden of a diocesan conference centre, a hospital chaplain, a community relations officer who is an expert on inter-faith matters, a community worker in a UPA parish, care of an old people's home, a diocesan youth officer working with the young homeless and a diocesan adviser for children's work.

168   A number of points emerged in response to the general question about how the role of Accredited Lay Workers is perceived. The first was that in a number of places his or her role is seen primarily as that of assisting the clergy. Elsewhere, emphasis is placed upon the specialist areas that can be undertaken by Accredited Lay Workers and the need to train them for a growing number of specialist posts. 'In future one hopes accredited lay ministry might develop along more imaginative lines transcending parochial boundaries and developing more specialist collaborative ministries.' At least three replies noted that at present there is a great similarity between their role and that of deaconesses. The hope is expressed by some that the ordination of women to the diaconate will open the way for a renewed emphasis on the value of professional lay ministry within the Church, a ministry which will be exercised by those trained in specific skills with 'less upfront' and 'less liturgical functions'. One reply suggests that 'we need to encourage those who wish to continue as Lay Workers that their particular ministry is important in the Church today.'

(3) DEACONESSES

169   The ordination since the completion of the questionnaire of more than 700 deaconesses and Accredited Lay Workers to the third

order of ministry significantly affects this study, in terms of the distribution of diaconal ministry between the categories of ordained and lay ministry. Understandably, there are differing views which reflect the uncertainty of the present situation, and the role of the deaconess is commonly seen as being identical to that of a deacon; e.g. 'Deacon(esse)s can undertake as wide a variety of ministries as priests, with the sole exception of sacramental function at present. We would not wish to retain this difference . . .' The functions carried out differ really only in regard to the permission given to deacons to officiate at marriage services. In answer to the questionnaires completed before these ordinations, all returns were from dioceses and episcopal areas which employed deaconesses. The diocese of Sodor and Man is the only diocese which has no deaconesses.

170   Deaconesses, like Accredited Lay Workers, are sometimes stipendiary, sometime non-stipendiary. The returns suggest that *in toto* there are approximately 448 stipendiary and 297 non-stipendiary deaconesses. The Stepney Area of the London diocese is alone in employing two *local* non-stipendiary deaconesses. The number of deaconesses in each diocese or area varies from one in a few dioceses to more than 20 in two dioceses. One-third of the dioceses and areas have between 10 and 20 stipendiary deaconesses. The considerable number of non-stipendiary deaconesses ranges from under five in 21 dioceses to more than 20 in two dioceses, the highest number being 34.

171   Selection is done entirely by the national ACCM procedure. All the training is either residential at a theological college or by a non-residential training scheme recognised nationally by the House of Bishops, and is identical to that for men to be ordained to the priesthood. The length of training is two to three years, in accordance with Bishops' Regulations. All the replies showed that training is funded from central church funds, though some dioceses said that diocesan funds are also used, as are LEA grants. The diocese of Europe was the only diocese to mention a student funding her own training.

172   After ordination, deaconesses are licensed or authorised to serve in a diocese, deanery or parish, the majority being appointed to a parish. Sometimes a licence is for two or more spheres of work. Increasingly, deaconesses are being licensed to special forms of

ministry as chaplains in colleges, universities, schools, hospitals, prisons or industrial mission; as teachers in theological colleges; as diocesan directors of lay ministry and for work with the Church Pastoral Aid Society.

173   The majority of dioceses give licences to deaconesses for an indefinite period, 14 for a limited period. Two dioceses mention retirement ages of 60 or 65 for stipendiary deaconesses and 70 for non-stipendiary. The Kensington Area of London has 20 deaconesses licensed for a period relating to the particular post and also mentions that those who have a 'retirement' ministry are reviewed annually. Some dioceses set fixed terms for specialist posts and in Portsmouth non-stipendiary ministers have a fixed title period of three years, after which licences are reviewed every five years. Southwark has contracts of three or five years and those with Permission to Officiate are subject to annual renewal. Conditions of service are governed by the Regulations for Non-Stipendiary Ministry, recently agreed by the House of Bishops.

174   Although by far the greatest number of deaconesses work in parochial ministry, an increasing number of specialist posts are opening up and the list is impressive. In addition to chaplaincies in industry, education, hospitals and prisons, the range includes diocesan communications officer, bishop's officer for social responsibility, diocesan director of ordinands, diocesan lay ministry adviser, dean of women's ministry, minister in a multi-faith situation, cathedral chaplain, chaplain to a city store, warden of readers, chaplain to a bishop and chaplain to a Christian conference centre.

175   Many interesting observations were made in answer to the question as to how the role of a deaconess is perceived, although it is clear that the majority of deaconesses will have been ordained to the diaconate by the end of 1987. One diocese made the point that it was unhappy to describe this as a 'permanent' diaconate. The hope was expressed that women would in the not too distant future be able to proceed to ordination to the priesthood. There were, however, those who shared a concern for discovering a distinctive role for those who will not be so ordained and 'not necessarily restricted to pastoral, liturgical or administration functions, not necessarily parish based and not always subsidiary to the incumbent'.

176   Many responses emphasise that the growing number of

deaconesses contributes to a much greater awareness of the role of women in ministry. 'Their role is becoming an important one in the diocese and both clergy and congregations come to appreciate and understand how much the ministry of women can mean. They play their full part in both deanery and diocesan affairs and have an increasing impact on the life of the diocese.' Another diocese adds that 'as the Church explores new patterns of ministry, women will be used increasingly in jobs with greater responsibility, i.e. doing similar work to that of a team vicar and looking after a daughter church.' The comments do not centre around arguments about priesthood for women, but rather about including more women within the professional, lay and ordained diaconal ministries. One diocese speaks of the pioneering role of women in ministry, another says that it is 'important that women be encouraged to discover their own contribution to the work of the Church rather than be conformed to the world of male patterns and masculine values.' Although there are dioceses which talk of women deaconesses as 'assistant staff', assisting the clergy or supporting the clergy, the most frequent emphasis is upon a ministry of service which is 'complementary' to that of the priest or 'alongside'.

177   The answers revealed much hopefulness and expectancy, as a greater number of women in particular are involved in the professional, full-time diaconal ministry. One diocesan bishop went as far as saying: 'we plan to ordain 14 deacons in July of whom eight will be women. This is a miracle!'

(4) CHURCH ARMY PERSONNEL

178   The total number of Church Army workers recorded in the replies is given as 193. Forty dioceses (or episcopal areas) have male stipendiary officers and 21 have female stipendiary officers, whilst seven dioceses have male non-stipendiary officers and nine dioceses have female non-stipendiary officers. The highest numbers of stipendiary workers in any diocese are nine in the case of men (two dioceses have this number) and five in the case of women (again, two dioceses have this number). The highest number of non-stipendiary officers in a single diocese is five, in the case of men, and three, in the case of women.

179   It should be noted, however, that the figures extracted from diocesan replies differ significantly from those provided by the Church

Army Headquarters. The latter include all officers in dioceses, whether they are licensed or not. Those without a licence may be inactive through bringing up children or working in a non-church setting. In one diocese at least only those working on a parochial staff receive a licence. The Church Army's own tables of figures are attached in Appendix 3.

180   Selection and two external assessments for ministry are carried out by the Church Army; assessors appointed by ACCM assist. The training course is approved by ACCM for the training of those selected for the Office of Evangelist and its length is either two or three years, depending on experience. Funding for training comes largely from Church Army sources, although LEA grants and parochial, diocesan and other trust funds are sometimes secured.

181   The majority of licences for work are to the parish, although there are places where licences are to diocesan or deanery posts. Other areas of work for which licences are given include prison work, wardens of hostels, work amongst the homeless, work at homes for the elderly, and a bishop's adviser on evangelism. In 27 dioceses the licences are for an indefinite period, whilst elsewhere a limit is set according to the specific work.

182   When asked about the forms of ministry in this group, 12 dioceses see it as general ministry and 13 emphasise specialised ministries in a variety of forms. Specialist areas held by Church Army personnel correspond in many instances to those covered by evangelism and the outreach of the Church's mission. Other specialist areas include rehabilitation work with men moving out of hostels, rural evangelism, residential care for the elderly, work with the homeless, local radio, drug abuse, community youth work, work with the mentally handicapped, unemployment officer. These particular specialist posts, together with the emphasis on evangelism, give a 'characteristic stamp' to the lay ministry exercised by the Church Army.

183   More than half the replies speak of general parochial ministry and some note a confusion of role (e.g. 'There seems to be confusion about the role of the Church Army in parishes: a few members are able to maintain their vision as an evangelist but this is increasingly difficult for many of the Captains who move into the ordained ministry as being the way in which they can more fully serve the

Church.') One diocese simply states 'very similar to a curate'. A number of replies mention diaconal ministry (e.g. '. . . would all own their primary role as being evangelists. In practice I suspect much of their ministry is to exercise a diaconal role.' ' . . . no distinctive role, but valued as lay and trained pastors, evangelists and preachers – could be seen as deacons if they chose to be').

184 'An Evangelist's role should emphasise ministry on the fringes and be in a mission context rather than being a substitute curate which conceals the particular specialism of the evangelist. More appropriate parishes and areas of ministry would seem to be in UPA areas and other "mission" areas rather than the leafy suburbs.' Whilst there are some Captains who feel drawn to the priesthood, and a few Sisters who are offering themselves for ordination as deacons, generally speaking this comment describes the work of Church Army personnel. Evangelism is understood as the primary ministry exercised in parish or diocesan situations, with expertise in rural evangelism or evangelism in urban priority situations. The other emphasis which is clear from the questionnaires is the role that the Church Army has in identifiable areas of deprivation, need and amongst those at risk. Church Army Captains and Sisters have a special role in 'understanding the human dilemma' and in 'bringing resources of the Gospel to meet the situation'.

(5) READERS

185 The office of Reader is exercised in many parts of the Anglican Communion. In the Church of England the ministry of the Reader is the only lay ministry which is essentially voluntary and governed by Canon. The number, both men and women, has increased considerably in recent years, so that there are over 7000 Readers and more than 1200 of them are women. This means that the number admitted to the office is approximately the same as the number ordained. All dioceses have Readers, both women and men. The highest number of male Readers in a single diocese is 300: the highest number of female Readers is 76. The diocese of Winchester alone differentiates between local (i.e. related to the parish) and diocesan Readers.

186 The great variety of procedures for selection, training and authorisation makes it difficult to summarise material relating to Readers. Unlike the three previous types of ministry, all selection for

Readers is done locally. A wide range of people are employed as selectors; sometimes candidates are interviewed by a panel, sometimes by a single selector. Some dioceses use an appointed Warden or Sub-Warden for Readers, or a Secretary or Registrar of the Diocesan Readers' Board. In three dioceses the bishop also interviews the candidates. Information which is sought in advance, to aid selectors, includes a written statement by the candidate, a pre-vocational course, a recommendation from the candidate's incumbent and the approval of the PCC. The diocese of Lichfield insists upon discussion with the incumbent and a subsequent review with the PCC of the candidate's work in the parish.

187   As to training, 28 of the dioceses use the General Readers' Course, with tuition usually given by individual tutors. Some dioceses combine the General Readers' Course with a diocesan-based scheme. Six dioceses use their own training programme. The diocesan courses vary in length and in the balance between group and individual work, formal lectures and one-to-one tutorials. Some dioceses include residential weekend training courses. The diocesan returns suggest that a great deal of work and thought goes into the training of Readers and in most dioceses the demands made on candidates are considerable, with training lasting from two to four years. Funds for training are largely diocesan, with some additional parochial support, and, in many places, students contribute to their own training.

188   The Reader's licence may be simply to the diocese, although it is more often to the parish. In six dioceses the licence is to the incumbent. The period of the licence differs. Whilst in six dioceses the licence is indefinite, other dioceses range from a term of one year to five. Sometimes a distinction is drawn between authorisation for an indefinite term and a licence for two or three years. Ten dioceses mention 70 as an age at which a Reader's ministry ought to be reviewed.

189   The focus of a Reader's work is most often described as 'general ministry', though some dioceses underline specialised ministries of preaching and teaching. Other specified tasks include liturgical duties, ministry to the sick, pre- and post-baptismal care, care and counselling of the bereaved, children and young people, and marriage preparation. Occasionally a Reader may be licensed to a particular sphere of work, to a public school or as a hospital or prison chaplain's assistant and in the Armed Services.

190   One diocese describes the role of the Reader as 'a non-stipendiary diaconal ministry' and many of the replies speak of role-confusion or of searching for a role, whilst about one-third mention pastoral ministry. However, at least half describe Readers in terms such as 'lay theologian', 'people taught to think theologically', 'theological resource people', 'people able to bring secular insights to bear on theology and theological insights to bear on secular concerns', 'those whose concern is with the interface of the Church and the work and the world and the Church'. This ministry of 'theological resource' is a unique and distinct ministry: the Reader is not a 'pseudo-clergyman' – he or she is essentially lay. Consistent with the notion of a 'theological resource person', the main tasks of the Reader are described over and over again as preaching and teaching. 'I see Readers as well-taught preachers of the Word authorised to take part in public worship and capable of expounding the Scriptures with a measure of maturity and spiritual discernment', wrote one bishop.

191   A few dioceses draw attention to an increasing pastoral ministry exercised by Readers in response to local needs and using the particular skills of the Reader. In some responses this is seen as a positive and welcome development, whilst in others a note of caution is sounded: it could lead to an ambiguity of roles amongst different diaconal ministries. In particular, one diocese mentions a threat to Lay Elders when a pastoral dimension to the ministry of Readers is emphasised.

192   What is also clear is that in areas where there is a shortage of clergy the Reader's role is invaluable. 'In rural areas Readers play an important role in maintaining an adequate round of services; in more urban areas the liturgical role may be much smaller though there is likely to be more opportunity for educational and pastoral work.' Not surprisingly, the diocese of Europe noted the important help Readers give in areas where there are few priests. There is some evidence that Readers are 'unevenly spread' in some dioceses and many of them emerge in parishes in 'middle-class areas'.

193   Some replies noted that the ministry of Readers is essentially a lay ministry and should remain so, without being drawn within an overarching diaconate. Readers have an important and proper place in the trained and recognised lay ministries of the Church and fit well into a period of church history where the emphasis is upon the

ministry of teams and groups. Here Readers can minister as 'theologically reflective' people alongside incumbents, as part of the parish ministry team with other specialised lay ministries.

(6) DISTINCTIVE DEACONS

194 Only seven dioceses (Birmingham, Bradford, Manchester, Oxford, Portsmouth, St Albans and Sheffield) had Distinctive Deacons at the time the questionnaire was circulated. The situation is dramatically altering in 1987, as women are being ordained to the diaconate. Birmingham and Manchester employ stipendiary deacons (one in each diocese), whilst three dioceses have one non-stipendiary deacon, St Albans two. Portsmouth has largely pioneered the renewal of a local permanent diaconate and now has seven Distinctive Deacons.

195 Three of the dioceses have sent their candidates to ACCM Selection Conferences. In Birmingham and Sheffield the diocesan bishop selected the candidates, whilst Portsmouth has a locally worked-out selection process which involves interviews with individuals, group exercises and a pastoral letter exercise. Again, training varies. In three cases the training has been a course recognised nationally by the House of Bishops, either at a theological college or on a non-residential course. In Birmingham a shortened form of the West Midlands non-residential training scheme has been used. In Portsmouth a two-year core curriculum in theology and a year's training course on ministerial formation makes a total of three years' training. Mostly the funds for training are from diocesan sources. Where a candidate is centrally selected and trained according to Bishops' Regulations, his or her training is funded by the Central Fund for Ordination Candidates.

196 The licence given for work is 'to the parish', until the age of 65 in Birmingham, indefinite in Bradford and Sheffield, whilst in Portsmouth it is for a three-year period in the first instance and then renewable at five-yearly intervals.

197 The work of the very few male Distinctive Deacons is described by Bradford and Portsmouth as 'general ministry', whilst in Birmingham are mentioned liturgical duties, administration, work with drug addicts and alcoholics; in Sheffield, care of the bereaved, ministry to the sick, liturgical duties and ministry to the wider community.

198 Responses to the question of the role of the distinctive diaconate range from a lack of enthusiasm to one diocese which says 'we await your report with interest' and others (in addition to those mentioned above) which are considering or already training Distinctive Deacons. The role of the deacons is described as 'unusual' or 'absolutely unique' and at least two dioceses claimed no intention of ordaining more. The only exception to this is Portsmouth: 'it is a general ministry aimed to focus the diaconal ministry/role of the Church. It is intended that deacons look outward to the wider community, but that there also be a liturgical focus too. They may be licensed to preach.'

(7) PASTORAL LAY MINISTERS

199 One of the forms of diaconal ministry to emerge in the last twenty years is that which can be placed under the general heading of 'pastoral lay ministry'. This includes Pastoral Lay Assistants, Lay Pastors, Lay Elders and Pastoral Workers. Eighteen dioceses have recognised Pastoral Lay Ministers, both women and men. Only two women are stipendiary. These ministers are best described as local, non-stipendiary lay ministers. The diocese of Wakefield has the largest number: 153 men and 322 women. Salisbury comes next with 152 men and 305 women; Winchester has 100 men and 300 women, Guildford 94 men and 250 women, and the diocese of St Edmundsbury and Ipswich 117 men and 96 women. Of the other dioceses with a significant number, these range from Blackburn with 18 men and 73 women to York with three men and four women.

200 The method of selection and training for Pastoral Lay Ministry varies greatly from diocese to diocese. An emphasis is placed on selection by the local parish community, articulated by the incumbent or by the incumbent and the PCC. In a number of cases a diocesan Lay Training Officer, Head Deaconess, or Rural Dean is involved in selection. Only Chester and the London area of London mention an interview with the bishop. Two dioceses have introduced a selection panel at diocesan level and Rochester runs a pre-vocational course before selection.

201 The length of training and its content differ widely. In two dioceses which use a non-residential, nationally recognised scheme, training lasts for three years; in four dioceses it is spread over two years. Everywhere else courses extend from three to 12 months. In three dioceses the training is left to the parish and the incumbent. In

Carlisle, if the Lay Pastoral Assistant is to carry out a preaching ministry, then (in addition to courses on pastoral, sacramental and liturgical subjects) the courses in theology taken by Readers are also used. Some dioceses have set up diocesan or deanery schemes. In Wakefield, for example, weekly evening sessions are spread over a year. Southwark includes two residential training weekends, reflection on biblical material, spirituality and ministry in regular group meetings, a one-week placement and a project; in addition, each student is required to have a spiritual director. The diocese of Rochester includes a course on worship, Christian ethics, pastoral care of the elderly and sick, parish and community projects, theology, hospital visiting and counselling; this course is run for groups, with shared academic and practical work.

202   Funding for training comes from diocesan funds, sometimes from parochial, sometimes from both. One diocese said it came entirely from students. The response from Wakefield probably sums up the haphazard and precarious nature of funding for this ministry: 'local organisers and session leaders are unpaid. Petty expenses are funded by selling coffee. The diocese supplies £12.50 per year in each of six centres for a library and pays for part of a diocesan organiser and secretarial and administrative back-up'.

203   Licences are given mostly to parishes. In five dioceses this is for an indefinite period of time, elsewhere it is mostly renewable every three years.

204   The focus of the work of local Pastoral Lay Ministers varies according to gifts. Although in some five dioceses 'general ministry' is given as the description, others mention only special tasks. Mostly these include pre- and post-baptismal care, care of the bereaved, marriage preparation and ministry to the sick; counselling, teaching, administration, and work with children and young people come next, with liturgical duties and preaching specified in only a few instances. A few Pastoral Lay Ministers work in spheres other than those within the parish, such as in hospital chaplaincies, industrial mission, evangelism and hospice care; one is mentioned as an ecumenical officer, another as a diocesan drama adviser.

205   It seems that the gifts of individuals are recognised and used as appropriately as possible. St Edmundsbury and Ipswich writes that 'each parish attempts to harness the Lay Elder's gifts for the specific ministry required. They are not licensed to preach, and there is a

great variety of ministry, mainly pastoral, with limited liturgical functions'. A different development is described in Southwark: 'This year (1987) we have started training Southwark Pastoral Auxiliaries to become "community workers".'

206 In answer to the question about the perceived role of the Pastoral Lay Ministers there was much enthusiasm and expectancy expressed in a large number of dioceses. Comments include the need to harness a much-needed resource of very varied talents by the identifying, training and recognising of these lay ministers. People of differing churchmanship, different social backgrounds and intellectual abilities are brought into recognised ministry, whilst many who are retired, unemployed or housewives have time and energy to devote to ministry. The result is a better trained, better equipped, abler laity ready to support and complement the work of the ordained clergy. The recruitment of lay ministers means that more visiting and more caring can be done in parishes, and it gives the whole parish a more credible witness. The Lay Ministers themselves feel that their gifts are being used.

207 Working in teams is seen as particularly appropriate for this kind of ministry. In the parish of X

a ministry team has developed for pastoral care and extended communion over the last six years. In 10 other parishes ministry teams are developing particularly for visiting and other forms of pastoral care. Such team members would be licensed for three years to serve in their own parish. In addition the majority of parishes in the diocese have two or three lay persons approved by the bishop for administering the chalice at Holy Communion. All these lay pastors are non-stipendiary, confined to their own parish and limited in their length of service . . . they are always seen as members of a team as opposed to being individually licensed in some quasi-professional manner.

208 In Guildford, Pastoral Assistants are firmly parochially based and commissioned, whilst in St Edmundsbury and Ipswich Lay Elders operate only in their own parish or benefice (with only a limited liturgical role which does not include preaching) and have no set training or job description; there is nevertheless an Annual Conference for all Lay Elders.

209 None of the comments from any of the dioceses hints at a threat to the ministry of every Christian by selecting and recognising Pastoral Lay Ministers. Although they do things that any lay person

might do, the various schemes in fact encourage 'every member ministry' and do not 'draw out an elite' over and against the rest. Southwark suggests that as 'representative' lay ministers 'they are in a very good position to help other laity'.

210 One diocesan bishop looking forward to the establishment of Pastoral Lay Ministers in his diocese says:

> This will be very important for us for we have little or no tradition of lay ministry here which I see as expressing (with priests and bishop) the totality of the Church's mission to the world, its pastoral care, its social witness, its liturgical work, and, above all, its converting task. We cannot go on as we are.

(8) SUMMARY AND COMMENT

211 The picture that emerges from the questionnaires is an impressive one. There is a great deal of activity and experiment in the area of diaconal ministry and there is much variation from diocese to diocese. However, from it all comes the impression that the diaconal ministry of the Church is 'on the move'. Within the total ministry of the whole people of God diaconal ministry relates both to the priests and to the bishops, assisting them and providing a complementary ministry. It relates also to the ministry of the 'non-professional' laity, providing examples, encouraging and enabling them. The answers to the questionnaire do not give the impression either that those in diaconal ministry are quasi-clergy or that the action identifying and training certain men and women stultifies the ministry of the whole people of God. A few clergy feel threatened by the newly-found and trained expertise of lay men and women, or by laity inappropriately seeking status, or where there appears to be a genuine confusion of roles. But the overall impression is of the recognition of tasks to be done and of the gifts and talents being identified and used in the service of the Church and in its mission.

212 *Accredited Lay Workers* and remaining *Deaconesses* are seen as professional lay ministers with the accent both on professional and lay. There is an emphasis on the number of specialist posts opening up for this group and a hope that more specific skills will be encouraged. It is possible that this group may respond particularly in future to 'gaps' identified in the caring of the Welfare State and respond to needs in urban priority areas. There is a clear recognition

of the value of professional lay ministry, both in terms of providing specialist expertise and also in enabling more Pastoral Lay Ministers.

213   The special concern of the *Church Army* is that of evangelism and caring in areas of risk and deprivation. It is recognised that within the total ministry of the Church evangelism should be underlined in the contribution of an identifiable group, not so much in order to take that function to themselves as to be examples of the vocation of all the baptised.

214   *Readers* provide a highly valued ministry with a very definite accent on lay people trained to think theologically and able to communicate. Many also have a pastoral role, but it is their theological expertise amongst the laity that seems characteristically the ministry of Readers.

215   *Distinctive Deacons* are seen as having a very similar role to the professional Accredited Lay Worker but stand within the ordained ministry and have additional liturgical functions. It remains unclear how this order will develop, as many of the women who now make up the order see their vocation ultimately as to a priestly and not to a diaconal ministry.

216   The recent development of *Pastoral Lay Ministers* suggests a start to the harnessing of untapped resources and the unfreezing of 'God's Frozen People'. Through the contribution of Pastoral Lay Ministers in many parishes, the responsibility of every Christian to serve can be encouraged.

217   It would be true to say that, in addition to some role confusion (among Readers and Church Army personnel) and role uncertainty (among Accredited Lay Workers), there is much overlap in the tasks carried out by the groups involved in recognised diaconal ministry. However, apart from a very few instances, this is not identified as a problem. For, in spite of the overlapping (liturgically, pastorally and in specialist ministries), there emerges a definite and recognisable emphasis within each different group.

218   Recent developments in diaconal ministry seem to be successful in maintaining a balance between establishing order for the right reasons (i.e. proper training and accreditation), and at the same time allowing for local diversity and local oversight to be exercised appropriately by the bishop. It is important that those in diaconal

ministry be seen in a special way as related to the ministry of the bishop.

219 Professionalism, too, is important in those who are recognised and representative ministers of the Church. So it is right that resources, both national and diocesan, should be spent on equipping women and men for ministry. The emergence of regional resources centred on existing theological colleges and non-residential courses is urgently needed and is essential in the preparation of men and women for ordained and lay ministry. Joint training whenever appropriate does much to establish the view that the Church's ministry is one, even if different people have different gifts in a variety of tasks, and opens the way for joint work in teams.

220 The answers to the questionnaires reveal how important are the developments in diaconal ministry for discovering the contribution that women in particular have to give to the professional ministry of the Church. Their participation in this ministry, irrespective of whether or not women should be ordained to the priesthood, is affirmed as bringing a complementarity and wholeness to ministry.

221 Concentration on what is happening in one area of ministry (whether diaconal, priestly, episcopal or of the laity) is open to the danger of obscuring the importance of the others and so of destroying the necessary balance of the whole. Recognised diaconal ministry needs to be seen within the total circle of the ministry of the Body of Christ, where it has a very special function in witnessing to the ministry of Christ, the Deacon who came not to be served but to serve.

5 The Diaconate in Ecumenical Dialogue[17]

(1) INTRODUCTION

222 There are two significant advances in the understanding of the ordained ministry in the multilateral and bilateral dialogues. The first is in the area of *episkope* and episcopacy; the second is in the understanding of the ordering of the ordained ministry. This second area includes the understanding of the diaconate.

223 All of the dialogues which treat of the ordained ministry do so in the context of the ministry of the whole people of God, a ministry which derives from the ministry of Christ. There is a necessary and close inter-relationship between the ministry of the ordained and that of the non-ordained. This is important to establish because it has consequences for the outworking of all ministry and relates to the functions of ministry which belong to all alike. While all the dialogues recognise that from the very beginning of the Church's life there were persons holding specific responsibility and authority, none of the dialogues maintains that the ordering of the distinctive ministry can be found in a New Testament blueprint.

(2) BAPTISM, EUCHARIST AND MINISTRY: THE LIMA TEXT

224 The *Lima Text* agrees that in the New Testament there is a variety of forms of ministry which existed at different places and times. Certain elements became settled in the second and third centuries into the threefold pattern. In succeeding centuries the ministry underwent considerable changes. The functions of ministry were distributed in different ways. The *Lima Text* does not mean to imply by this that it was only after the Reformation that changes were made. In the early centuries the role of the bishop changed from being leader of a single eucharistic community to being leader of an area. As a consequence of the change in the role of the bishop, the roles of presbyter and deacon also changed. In particular, the deacons (as assistants of the bishop) received responsibilities in a wider area.

225   Although the pattern of ministry has been a changing one, the *Lima Text* is nevertheless clear that 'the three-fold ministry of bishop, presbyter and deacon *may* serve today as an expression of the unity we seek and also as a means of achieving it'. This is because it became the generally accepted pattern in the early Church and because it is still retained by many churches today. It serves to express the necessary diaconal, presbyteral and episcopal aspects of ministry.

226   However, in the churches that retain it, the threefold order is in need of reform. The *Lima Text* mentions two places where reform is needed. The first is at the level of the eucharistic community, where the collegial dimension of leadership has suffered. Then with regard to deacons, where they do exist, they have been reduced to having an assistant role in the liturgy and no longer function in the diaconal witness of the Church.

227   When the *Lima Text* comes to discuss the functions of the deacons it says:

> *Deacons* represent to the Church its calling as servant in the world. By struggling in Christ's name with the myriad needs of societies and persons, deacons exemplify the interdependence of worship and service in the Church's life. They exercise responsibility in the worship of the congregation; for example, by reading the scriptures, preaching and leading the people in prayer. They help in the teaching of the congregation. They exercise a ministry of love within the community. They fulfil certain administrative tasks and may be elected to responsibilities for governance (M31).

228   The *Lima Text*, then
affirms a threefold order

sees the diaconate in need of reform

understands the interplay between service and worship as characteristic of diaconal vocation

suggests that deacons may be elected to positions of responsibility

sees that deacons have a special relationship to the bishop.

There are some challenges here for Anglicans, particularly in the need for the diaconal role to link service to the world with liturgical functions, and for the need for positions of responsibility to be open to deacons. If those Churches (as in the Anglican Communion) which have retained the threefold order are to commend that order in ecumenical dialogue, there is need for a more credible expression of the diaconate.

(3) THE *FINAL REPORT* OF THE ANGLICAN–ROMAN CATHOLIC INTERNATIONAL COMMISSION

229   ARCIC recognises that while there were 'normative principles' governing the purpose and function of the ministry already present in the New Testament, there was 'a considerable diversity of structure'. It likens the emergence of the threefold ministry to the Canon of Scripture: it was incomplete until the second half of the second century. As the dialogue is between two Churches which claim to have a threefold order, there is no attempt to justify it. Neither is there any suggestion of the need for change or reform, which seems odd in the light of the current developments in both the Churches involved. A statement in ARCIC on the necessity for reform of the diaconate might have had some relevance not only for Anglicans and Roman Catholics, but for those Churches challenged by the *Lima Text* to consider moving in the direction of a threefold order, for the sake of unity.

230   All that is said about deacons is that, although they are not empowered (as presbyters are) to preside at the eucharist and pronounce absolution, they are 'associated with bishops and presbyters in the ministry of word and sacrament, and assist in oversight' (Ministry, 9). After this paragraph the deacon falls into the background and, in talking in general terms about the 'part of ministers' and the 'responsibility of ministers', the text speaks only about bishops and presbyters.

(4) *GOD'S REIGN AND OUR UNITY:* THE ANGLICAN–REFORMED DIALOGUE

231   It is particularly interesting to note what this dialogue has to say about the diaconate, as it is between a Church that has retained a threefold order at the Reformation and others which have not.

232   The statement follows closely the *Lima Text* and focuses on three things:

> (i) The particular ministerial structures which are now embodied in our different communions cannot claim the direct authority of Scripture. The New Testament cannot be held to prescribe a three-fold ministry of

bishops, priests and deacons, a presbyterian or congregational form of government, or the primacy of the see of Rome. All attempts to read off one divinely authorized form of ministry from the New Testament are futile.

(ii) The Church is a living body which should combine continuity of tradition with adaptation to new situations under the guidance of the Holy Spirit.

(iii) Not all the developments of the past nineteen centuries are to be regarded as divinely sanctioned simply because they have occurred . . . nor to be rejected because they are not explicitly authorized by Scripture. Our duty is first to receive and cherish them with gratitude, and then to learn, as those before us have done, to adapt and reform them under the guidance of the Spirit in faithfulness to the apostolic witness, and in accordance with the missionary needs of our day. (77)

233 In the lengthy statement on ordination the discussion links ordination with the celebration of the eucharist. 'Ordained person' here seems exclusively to refer to the person who is the president of the eucharist.

234 However, when the text proceeds to talk about the shape of the ministry, it clearly favours the re-emergence of a threefold pattern. It cannot claim to be the *only* pattern sanctioned by the New Testament, but it eventually prevailed and was generally adopted and is accepted by the large majority of Christians to-day. It 'should be accepted in some form for the sake of the unity and continuity of the Church, both locally and universally, and for the sake of its missionary calling' (92).

235 The text proceeds to show how the pattern has been deformed in both Churches. Both have tended to reduce the three orders to two. The text suggests that whilst the Reformed Churches need to consider recovering the episcopal ministry, Anglicans need to rediscover the diaconate and to bring deacons into collegial relation with the presbyters in the local church; this would be the counterpart of the pastor surrounded by a group of elders and deacons in most churches in the Reformed tradition.

(5) SUMMARY

236 There is much congruity in the three dialogues and this can be summarised as follows

The three dialogues all favour the retention and reformation of a threefold order but never on the grounds that this was *the* pattern of ministry laid down in the New Testament.

The role of the deacon is seen primarily in terms of the local church, though the *Lima Text* does mention wider responsibilities.

Although the deacon in the early Church was primarily associated with the bishop, this is not picked up in the dialogues. There is, however, reference in ARCIC to the sharing in episcopal oversight. It is the bishop who ordains the deacon, thus sharing with him his own authority.

The deacon is seen to be the one, according to the *Lima Text*, who pre-eminently unites service to the world and liturgical functions, and thus embodies a way of life of coming to the liturgy and returning to the world, and in so doing exemplifies a pattern of living for all Christians.

Part Two

THEOLOGY

6   A Theology of the Diaconate

(1) INTRODUCTION

237   Inasmuch as theology draws upon Scripture, tradition, history and contemporary experience, a brief summary of the material given hitherto in this Report is provided by way of introduction.

238   In the early Church, deacons stood alongside the presbyterate/ episcopate as a separate order. However, in subsequent centuries the growth of a *cursus honorum* (where a deacon is seen to be at the foot of a ladder and the bishop at the top) accompanied a clear diminution of the significance of deacons. At the Reformation, whilst the reformed Churches reaffirmed the diaconal aspect of ministry and deacons worked amongst the poor and (later) in stewardship, the Church of England took over the medieval Catholic use of the diaconate, so that almost all deacons remained such often only for a matter of weeks, as an apprenticeship to the priesthood.[18] In the nineteenth century insistence on observing the BCP rubric meant that this period was extended to a year and there would always have been some ordained deacons who would have been under the minimum age for the priesthood. However, it was not until well into this century that a distinctive role for deacons came once again to be emphasised.

239   In other churches the pattern has varied. The deacon's liturgical role has been paramount in the Orthodox Church, whilst the German Evangelical Church has stressed the deacon's role in social care. Revival of the diaconate in the Roman Catholic Church has placed much stress on community work, especially in Germany and the USA, and similar emphases have been identified in parts of the Anglican Communion (notably in Southern Africa and in the Episcopal Church of the United States).

240   Within the Church of England, questionnaires have shown the present situation in diaconal ministry (outside the ordained diaconate) to be very mixed. Once again, however, pastoral work (both within the Church community and in the wider community) combined with some form of liturgical role, has been prominent in the replies from the dioceses on various diaconal ministries. This same

understanding is repeated in the *Lima Text* where a liturgical role is combined with community service.

241 A picture is presented by the evidence of the deacon (or diaconal ministries, more widely understood) playing a part in the reconciling activity of God within the wider community which finds its focus in the liturgy. God's reconciling activity is offered to the world through the diaconal, serving, self-giving aspect of the Church's ministry.

(2) THE NATURE OF *DIAKONIA*

242 The source and pattern for the diaconal aspect of the Church's ministry, as indeed for all ministry in the Church, is the ministry of Christ. Through the writings of the New Testament we gain our earliest picture of how the ministry, death and passion of Jesus were interpreted by the early Church: that the Church must live out this same ministry if it was to witness to the kingdom of God.

243 Jesus himself was born into a tradition, classically recorded in the Old Testament, where the God of Israel is personally involved with his creation. God invites his children to a shared involvement in his world. The recent report of the Doctrine Commission picks up this theme: 'Through the history of his people, God has been working out his purpose of creating a people capable of responding to his gracious will, and this is not for the sole benefit of Israel alone, but for all the peoples on earth.'[19] It is this same God whom Jesus addressed as Father, and whose work he manifested in his ministry. This ministry, together with the death and resurrection of Jesus, is seen by Paul as the work of reconciliation which supremely brings to completion the promises of the old covenant and so restores communion.

244 The reconciling activity of God is a central stand in the various books of the Old and New Testaments. Genesis, in its account of the fall, describes humanity as having become alienated from God and this in turn produces alienation between human beings. God strives, however, through the establishment of a covenant to restore communion and the Old Testament writers describe in a number of ways God's reconciling activity.

245 The early pages of Scripture depict God giving himself to the act of creation (and resting from it in Gen. 2.2) and thereafter calling out a people with whom to establish a covenant. Despite Israel's

faithlessness, he moves repeatedly to restore the covenant relationship. Thus in the Old Testament the God who makes a covenant with his people Israel reveals himself as a God who keeps faith with an elect but erring nation. The picture is one of God creating us for communion, our constantly breaking that communion and his willing to restore it by reconciling humanity to himself and also human beings one to another.

246   It is into this background that Jesus was born and against it his ministry is to be interpreted. In the New Testament writings the work of reconciliation is classically expressed as the writers reflect on the life, death and resurrection of Jesus Christ, and their description of God's reconciling activity in Christ becomes the supreme pattern for all Christian ministry.

247   The serving, self-giving aspect of God's reconciling activity is crystallised in the New Testament in the concept of *diakonia*. This is given powerful expression in the 'Christ-hymn' in the Letter of Paul to the Philippians (Phil. 2.5-11). The significance of Christ's self-offering is emphasised in the use of the word *doulos*, which in other contexts is translated as 'slave'. Whether this hymn was in use in pre-Pauline Christian community worship (as many scholars argue), or whether it is actually Pauline, it is undeniably early and has great significance for Paul. For its seven verses are a crucial starting-point for a discussion of his doctrine of Christ within Christian theology. The hymn included the Greek work *ekenosen*, meaning 'emptied', and this is applied to Jesus in verse 7.

248   Similar thought patterns present themselves elsewhere in Paul's writings, and are implied when Paul describes God's activity as turning the world's values on their head. For example, in the First Letter to the Corinthians, Christ's crucifixion is presented as the 'foolishness' of God (1 Cor. 1.26-31); such a doctrine is a surprise to 'the world' and this is the example that all Christians are to follow and use as the basis for their own lives. Similar nuances are found in the letter to the Romans (Rom. 5.6-11). Pauline thought is inescapably impregnated with a picture of Jesus as the serving, self-giving one who shows to us the true nature of God, and so his example and God's act of grace must have implications for all Christians in their manner of life and in their ministry. It is thus that Paul develops his thought.

249   Whilst he has his own theological categories and patterns of

thought, Paul is not alone or idiosyncratic in his approach. For in the gospel tradition there are similar understandings, albeit clothed in different images and in a different literary genre. Mark's gospel is generally agreed to be the earliest of the synoptic writings and modern critical methods have heightened our awareness of the elements of self-giving, suffering and service in that gospel. It is easy to see how central the suffering of Jesus is to Mark and almost one-third of the gospel comprises the passion narrative. The first reference to Jesus' inevitable passion and death appears as early as chapter 3(v.6) and later Jesus predicts that he will be mocked, scourged and killed (8.31; 9.31; 10.33). The life of the one who reflects the true nature of God must reflect his servanthood and self-giving, and in the case of Jesus this can mean one thing only, death. The significance of this is set out in chapter 10, where Jesus is approached by James and John; it is made very clear by Jesus that they will share the same baptism as he, but it will not be quite what they expect. The key verses are 43-45: 'But it shall not be so among you; but whoever would be great among you must be your servant *(diakonos)*, and whoever would be first among you must be slave *(doulos)* of all. For the Son of man also came not to be served *(diakonethenai)* but to serve *(diakonesai)*, and to give his life as a ransom for many.' The 'diaconal' life of the Christian community takes its pattern from the life of the Son of man, who shows most clearly the nature of God on earth, and this is contrasted sharply in Mark's gospel with the life of the world.

250 It would be possible to go through the other two synoptic gospels showing how they illustrate this diaconal work of Jesus in their own particular ways. Suffice it to say that, despite their own distinctive witness, both Matthew and Luke inherit the strong strand of his self-giving which is present in Mark, whom they use as their point of origin. Furthermore, in the synoptic narratives, Jesus' service is not only of humanity, but service to the Father. The Gethsemane scene provides a powerful illustration of this, as Jesus offers himself up to the will of the Father (Luke 22.41-42).

251 John's gospel springs from a different tradition and his theology and imagery are different again. Nevertheless, the same double aspect of service is identifiable: Jesus' will and the will of the Father are one and the same (John 6.38), yet Jesus has come to serve humanity as well. Although the term itself is not used, the element of *diakonia* remains, and although cognate words appear in only two places in the

gospel, one of these is highly significant. In chapter 12 (v.26) Jesus says: 'If anyone serves *(diakone)* me, he must follow me; and where I am, there shall my servant *(diakonos)* be also; if anyone serves *(diakone)* me, the Father will honour him.' This immediately follows the passage which notes '. . . unless a grain of wheat falls into the earth and dies, it remains alone; but if it dies, it bears much fruit' (12.24). Here, once again, self-giving, suffering and service are linked both with him who most supremely reveals the nature of God to the Christian community, and with them who are exhorted to follow his example. In the following chapter this teaching is reinforced by the most vivid of acted parables in the washing of the disciples' feet, a parable of the way in which the Son of God loved his own to the uttermost.

252   One of the most significant sources for images relating to the diaconal work of Jesus stands in the Old Testament, in the Suffering Servant songs of Isaiah. It would be wrong to seek for diaconal patterns within Isaiah itself, but certainly these passages influenced the New Testament writers, as they sought to understand the true nature of Jesus, and his reconciling work within the providence of God.

253   Thus, in a variety of ways and through a wealth of different writings, the same point is pressed home: that one of the attributes of God manifest in Jesus Christ is that of *diakonia*, of self-emptying, of service, of suffering with and for his people. This same ministry of *diakonia* is entrusted to the Church which is the fruit of the incarnation, and all Christian people are called to fashion their lives, both individually and corporately, on God as revealed in Jesus Christ. It is the Church as a whole which is diaconal as well as priestly and which shares *episkope*. Individual ministers represent and focus these different facets within the Church and to the world.[20] All ministry in the New Testament has *diakonia* as its root word and it carries many nuances of meaning. It can be translated as 'service' and its cognate word *diakonos* (deacon) as 'servant'.

(3) *DIAKONIA* AND MINISTRY

254   In the New Testament, then, the root word for all ministry is *diakonia*. The Pauline concept of baptism into the death and resurrection of Christ (Rom. 6.5) emphasises the element of costly service for all God's people and they are reminded of it at every

81

Eucharist. Whilst in recent years there has been a rediscovery of the truth that ministry belongs to the whole Church and not only to those who are ordained, it has been pointed out that as a result, ministry has become a 'greedy concept'[21] and can swallow up all into its digestive system. There remains the need to distinguish between the ministry of the whole Church and, within that, the ministry of those 'called out' and ordained as sacramental ministers. Together these form the organic life of the Church.

255   However, as Bishop Stephen Bayne wrote, 'There is only one ministry – Christ's ministry. He is the only minister there is in the Church.'[22] For the Church, and for individual ministers within the Church, this demands that we participate in *diakonia* which embodies the characteristic suffering, redeeming life of Christ. As Paul writes in his First Letter to the Corinthians, 'When reviled, we bless; when persecuted, we endure; when slandered, we try to conciliate; we have become, and are now, as the refuse of the world, the offscouring of all things' (1 Cor. 4.12b–13).

256   The most thorough discussion of ministry in the New Testament is by Paul in his Second Letter to the Corinthians, where there appear to be references both to the wider ministry of the whole Church and to specific ministers within that ministry. In this context, the question remains as to what exactly Paul understands ministry to be. A clue to this is found in 2 Cor. 3.9, where Paul writes, 'For if there was splendour in the dispensation of condemnation, the dispensation of righteousness must far exceed it in splendour.' The ministry with which the Church is entrusted is a ministry of righteousness. This word takes us to the heart of Paul's thought and, indeed, returns us to its roots in the Old Testament. For righteousness is what God hopes to establish with his people Israel and it is through the covenant established by his free grace that humanity may receive righteousness, and thus be reconciled with God. Issuing from this is a renewed relationship for the people of Israel with each other.

257   Paul sees this reconciliation as having happened through the death and resurrection of Jesus Christ, for in this, once and for all, God has established a right relationship with all humanity. It is the responsibility of each individual, and of the community as a whole, to accept and to stand open to this offer, and the ministry of the Church is there to assist all humanity in appropriating this reconciliation. The ordained ministry has its part to play, although it is 'Not to undertake

some specialist activity from which the rest of the faithful are excluded, but to pioneer in doing that which the whole Church must do'.[23] It is the ordained ministry's aim to assist the Church in living a life fashioned upon God, and through its example to bring others to the gospel.

258   There is some difficulty in ascertaining when Paul is referring to the whole Church and when he is referring to those with a specific ministerial role. 2 Cor. 5.16–19 is a key passage where Paul is almost certainly speaking of the ministry of all Christians. In verse 18 he writes: 'All this is from God, who through Christ reconciled us to himself and gave us the ministry *(diakonia)* of reconciliation'. Here *diakonia* is used in its root sense, and the word is used in a similar manner in 2 Cor. 4.1. Likewise, the term *diakonos* should not be read as 'deacon' in any technical sense as a minister in these chapters (2 Cor. 6.4). For Paul is referring to the commission placed upon the entire Church and the force of the terms *diakonia* and *diakonos* is to associate this commission with the life of Christ. Paul seeks to describe the sort of community the Church is called to be.

259   The sense in which 'ministry' is being used by Paul develops in 2 Cor. 5.20–21, and in using the term 'ambassadors' (5.20) it is most likely that he is referring to 'the ministry'. Still, however, there is the central concept of participation in the ministry of Christ and these passages centre on the ministry of reconciliation. At the root of this lies the issue of righteousness, for it is the 'putting right' of humanity with God which has effected reconciliation. This reconciliation is made present and effective in and for the Church and to the world by means of ministry.

260   The following section (2 Cor. 6.1–10) begins with a link passage and then leads into the famous rhetorical description of the life of the minister. Both *diakonia* and *diakonoi* appear in verses 3 and 4 and here Paul is almost certainly narrowing down the description to himself and his fellow workers. The passage is a vivid picture of what it means to live the life of *diakonia* and it rounds off Paul's single most concerted attempt to describe what ministry is about.

261   These chapters cannot be used simply to set out a prototype, on a practical level, for ministry at all times and in all ages. For Paul is attempting to show the relationship of the continuing life of the Christian community, and the work of its ministers, with the life,

death and resurrection of Jesus Christ. He is also concerned with what that says of God's relationship with all of humanity. It is a portrayal of ministry on a grand scale and on a wide canvas. What becomes clear in the process, however, is that the task of all ministry is participation in the ministry of Christ.

262   This ministry and its accompanying gifts are granted through the risen and ascended Christ, noted classically in Eph. 4.7ff: 'But grace was given to each of us according to the measure of Christ's gift. Therefore it is said, "When he ascended on high he led a host of captives, and he gave gifts to men." . . . And his gifts were that some should be . . .'

263   This argument reinforces the point that has been established earlier on, that Christ's ministry is determinative of all ministry. The life of the early Church witnesses to their attempt to live out this ministry. They did this both within the Christian community, and by what they proclaimed to the world through their life and their activity. In the course of time this came to be focused and expressed through an ordered ministry, but an ordered ministry which existed within rather than apart from the wider community of believers. The ordering of that ministry within a threefold pattern was expressive of the various elements of the ministry of Christ. His ministries, particularly those of oversight, of high priesthood and of service, are focused within three orders, although there have been from the beginning some overlap and interweaving of their various elements.

(4) FROM *DIAKONIA* TO DEACON

264   Whilst the term *diakonos* is used in 2 Corinthians in the general sense of ministry, sometimes it refers to the entire Christian community (who in that sense are deacons), and elsewhere it refers to those with a particular apostolic task. It does not refer to a 'deacon' in the technical sense. Equally, there is no evidence to suggest that Paul refers to an order of deacons in Phil. 1.1, where the letter is addressed to 'all the saints in Christ Jesus who are at Philippi, with the bishops *(episkopoi)* and deacons *(diakonoi)*', for the reference is almost certainly to the 'bishops and other church workers'.

265   A good deal has been made in the past of the appointment of 'the seven' in Acts (6.1–6) to serve at tables. These have been seen as proto-deacons and so as the foundation of the diaconate. There is no

evidence, however, to support this claim and it is likely that this is an idealised account, since the problem of practical help is likely to have been posed far earlier in the life of the Church than is here described. Furthermore, the later careers of Stephen and Philip hardly match the picture of the diaconate as it developed in the second and third centuries. In this passage the term *diakonia* is used in its most ordinary sense, and so the translation 'to serve tables' ought to be read in that light.

266   The only place in the New Testament where it is clear that the term *diakonos* means 'deacon' is in the Pastoral Epistles: 'Deacons likewise must be serious, not double-tongued, not addicted to much wine, not greedy for gain; they must hold the mystery of the faith with a clear conscience' (1 Tim. 3.8–9). Although this writer can still use the word in a general sense (1 Tim. 4.6), there is evidence here that, by the time these letters came to be written, an institutional form of ministry had started to develop in the embryonic Christian Church.

267   Certainly in sub-apostolic times this development continued and was accompanied by the beginnings of theological reflection. Similar sentiments to those in 1 Timothy are expressed in the letter of Polycarp to the Philippians: 'Deacons should be irreproachable in the face of God's justice, as the servants *(diakonoi)* of God and Christ and not of men. They should not be slanderous, not double-tongued, no lovers of money' (5.2). Furthermore, Ignatius, in his letter to the Magnesians (a little before Polycarp) writes: 'I bid you do everything in godly concord, with the bishop presiding in the likeness of God, with the presbyters in the likeness of the council of the apostles, while the deacons who are so dear to me have been entrusted with the ministry *(diakonia)* of Christ' (6.1). Bishops and deacons are to fashion themselves respectively upon God and Christ and this is further developed by Ignatius in his letter to the Trallians: 'Similarly all should respect the deacons as they would respect Jesus Christ, just as they should respect the bishop as the symbol of the Father and the presbyters as the senate of God and the assembly of the apostles: apart from these the Church is not called the Church' (Trall. 3.1).

268   So it would appear that the threefold ministry arose through the interplay of theological determinants and a response to need. For between Paul and the Pastoral Epistles and Ignatius there is a clear move toward more institutional forms of ministry. Yet it is remarkable that theological considerations play so significant a part in Ignatius'

description of their role and character. The Pauline emphasis issuing from the wider meaning of *diakonia* is retained and, as in Paul, ministry is rooted in Christ and, through Christ, in God. The deacon is an image of Christ. Thus it is not surprising that in Justin Martyr's Apology (mid-second century) deacons are given a position of primary significance in admitting each of the congregation to communion at the eucharist and taking communion to those who are absent (Apol. 1.65).

269   Following on from this reference to Justin and before leaving this early period, it is worth noting how the theological implications were worked out in practice. Although few details are given before the third century, the Shepherd of Hermas in the mid-second century refers to the social and welfare work of the deacon. The first full account, however, appears in the *Didascalia Apostolorum,* a third-century document probably of Syrian or Palestinian provenance. In this treatise, the deacon again stands in the place of Christ, and as no one can approach God except through Christ (the author argues), so Christians should approach the bishop through the deacons. The deacon therefore becomes the bishop's ear and alongside this are included some social and welfare work, together with the visiting of the sick. Liturgically, the deacon's main concern is with keeping order in the congregation: preventing heretics from attending the eucharist, making announcements and giving instructions during corporate worship. Other writers, notably Justin Martyr (Apol. 1.65.5) and Hippolytus (Ap. Trad. 16.25), supplement these duties with other liturgical tasks. These include administering communion, preparing the gifts, proclaiming the gospel, and proclaiming the *Exsultet* at Easter. Cyprian allows *(Letters* 18.1) for the deacon to pronounce an absolution, in extreme urgency, and other witnesses suggest that the deacon had responsibility for organising (rather than giving) catechesis.

270   The picture that builds up, then, in the second and third centuries is one of the deacon with a clearly defined liturgical role which is linked to works of welfare and social service in the community. Continuing to run alongside this is a responsibility for certain administrative tasks within the Church.

271   From all this early evidence, a picture is presented which is based upon 'being' and 'doing'. Whilst in New Testament times the

terms *diakonos* and *diakonia* were root words for ministry, they still raise vital questions about the nature of the ministers the Church needs if it is to be the body of Christ. Those ministers were described (in 2 Cor. 6.3–10) both by their activity and also by their 'being', and in the period of the Fathers this twin emphasis remained equally vivid. The insights of the early Christian community continued to be crucial wherever the Church was to live out with integrity the authentic marks of the gospel and they raise sharp questions for understandings of ministry in the contemporary world. Bishop Mark Santer writes: 'The deacon's duty and office is this: that he is entrusted with Christ's ministry to his people. Not the ministry of Christ the Shepherd, the priest or the Lord; but the ministry of Christ the servant of us all; the ministry without which all other ministry ceases to be Christlike ministry.'[24]

(5) FROM THE FATHERS TO THE PRESENT DAY

272   This understanding of God's nature and its links with Christian ministry continued into the later life of the Church. The early martyrdom of Polycarp and the later martyrdoms under the various persecutions, together with the early Christian tradition of 'baptism in blood', had shown that Christians were prepared to die for their faith, and so to emulate their Saviour. In a less extreme manner, the tradition survived in the monastic life and received new emphasis with the establishment of the orders of mendicant friars in the thirteenth century, notably Francis of Assisi who remained a deacon all his life.

273   Such a pattern of life, however, was by no means universal, and at times medieval Church polity obscured the diaconal strand within the Church's ministry. Some of the detailed reasons for this have already been set out in the historical section of this Report. Alongside this lesser emphasis on *diakonia* in the life of the Church, theologically it was a strand which received less attention at certain points in the medieval and later periods, although it would be wrong to claim that it was totally ignored.

274   The theological theme was pursued, however, with increasing vigour in the mid- to late nineteenth century. Within that period probably the most significant figure was Charles Gore who, in his Bampton Lectures of 1891, attempted to produce a reasoned

understanding of the doctrine of Christ. He returned to Phil. 2.5–11 and tried to show how we could better understand Jesus' ability to embrace humanity with divinity through an appreciation of God's self-emptying.[25] His attempts were criticised, but they set in train a renewed interest in this pattern of thought, and, with the loss of confidence in human progress caused by the First World War, theologians once again began to emphasise the self-emptying of God in Christ.[26]

275   The recent report of the Doctrine Commission referred to earlier is also concerned with this theme. It notes at one point: '[The] incarnate experience, with its intense joy as well as its depth of suffering, is our supreme clue to the mystery of God's relation to suffering as God, but it is not a direct picture of that relation.'[27] Elsewhere, reflecting on a related theme, the Anglican theologian (and member of that Commission), W. H. Vanstone, has argued for a re-ordering of our understanding of God which places self-giving and kenosis more prominently in our appreciation of the divine nature. Although not all would agree, Vanstone argues that what we see of God in Jesus is true of God throughout time. He writes: 'The "emptiness" of the Redeemer, in the poverty and humility of his historical existence, will point to the "emptiness" of God in and through his eternal activity.'[28] Moreover, Vanstone indicates that this has crucial significance for our understanding of the Church and for our appreciation of her work, as he writes: 'The Church lives at the point where the love of God is exposed to its final possibility of triumph or tragedy – the triumph of being recognised as love, the tragedy of so passing unrecognised that the final gift, the gift of which all other gifts are symbols, the gift of love itself is never known.'[29] The force of his argument is that the very nature of God revealed in Christ places upon the Church and its ministry an undeniable responsibility to reflect the nature of the divine in the world.

276   The picture that has been built up from Scripture, from the tradition, and from some of the writings of contemporary theologians, is consistent. The concept of costly *diakonia* remains a central strand in our understanding of the God worshipped through Jesus Christ. Alongside that has been identified the responsibility of the community who worship that same God to live that same life. Christian people are called to fashion their lives after the manner of the God they worship. Self-giving service is the pattern of his life.

(6) POINTERS TO *DIAKONIA* AND *DIAKONOS* IN THE CONTEMPORARY CHURCH

277 Much of the foregoing discussion has centred on the evidence from both Scripture and the tradition of the Church. In a historically rooted faith and community this is essential. However, it is equally important to relate this to the contemporary world and to bring its insights into dialogue with the tradition which has been examined, with reference to the Church's ministry.

278 Some twenty years ago the Church lost substantial numbers of priests to various forms of social work within the wider community. Alongside this, there was pressure from laity and clergy alike for the Church to focus more effectively on its role as servant of the world, in a rebellion against its continuing preoccupation with its own internal problems. There was a call to the Church to return to the servant/ social witness which it had fulfilled down the ages,[30] as exemplified in the mendicant friars, in its work in the Middle Ages in hospices and almshouses, and in its pioneering of the expansion of education, health and social service in nineteenth-century Britain. Whilst, in retrospect, it is easy to criticise the motivation behind some of its work, the fact remains that the Church had been committed to a strong emphasis on service. The rebellion of the 1960s by laity and priests was partly fuelled by more general social trends, but criticisms could not have been marshalled with such force had the Church remained clearly committed to an outward-looking servant role.

279 This servant role is important also as one means of establishing the position of the Church as a 'sign of the Kingdom'. The Church is not the Kingdom, but, when it acts authentically, it is a sign to the world of what God promises for all creation, as the Second Vatican Council describes it, 'the initial budding forth' of God's Kingdom. A commitment to work in the community, focused and encouraged in the ministry of the deacon, is an effective sign of the Kingdom and a reminder and proclamation of the Church's primary role as servant.

280 In the light of all this, it is significant that a variety of ministries has burgeoned in the Church in the last twenty years. The questionnaire relating to this Report (and completed by all the dioceses in the Church of England) reinforces this point well. The number of women offering for deaconess (now deacon) ministry has increased fourfold in the past ten years. The number of Readers has also grown

enormously, and many have seen in that ministry an outlet for their gifts as pastors rather than as potential teachers and preachers; thus, a ministry which originated as one of teaching and preaching has been stretched, in an attempt to include pastoral elements for which it was never intended. Perhaps most interesting of all has been the growth in schemes for training what the questionnaire called 'Pastoral Lay Ministers'. These are so varied as to defy common description, but they range from Pastoral Auxiliaries in some dioceses to Lay Elders in others. Some are trained and licensed through a diocesan scheme, whilst others are trained within the parish, with some sort of diocesan authorisation. Most of their ministry is pastoral in orientation, with little or no teaching, and many of these ministers have at least a minimal liturgical role. These developments have occurred alongside the other traditional 'diaconal ministries' of Church Army Officers and Accredited Lay Workers.

281   Whilst this growth of varied diaconal ministries is to be welcomed, and over-systematisation is to be avoided, some issues need to be faced. For example, the Pastoral Lay Ministers remain *ad hoc* and there is little relationship between the varying schemes across diocesan boundaries. This could raise difficulties where someone has exercised a considerable ministry which is not recognised in a move to another diocese. Moreover there is the question of how such functional ministries relate to the theological nature and task of the Church. For there would seem to be little or no understanding of these 'diaconal' ministries as focusing Christ's diaconal ministry through the Church, whereas ordination calls out individuals to represent both Christ to the Church and, through that, the Church's ministry in Christ to the world. This is certainly not to suggest that all lay ministers should be ordained deacon, but maybe we should ask whether the situation does not point to the need for a restored 'distinctive diaconate', for some of these ministers might well be candidates for ordination to that order.

282   A further source of evidence is to be found in material on the diaconate, both from other Churches and from Churches elsewhere in the Anglican Communion. The experience of Kaiserswerth and the existence of deacons of different sorts within the Reformed Tradition and the renewal of the diaconate both in the Roman Catholic Church and in other provinces of the Anglican Communion are all significant. Different visions exist alongside each other, but they testify to an

experience similar to that of the Church of England: that there is a need for an effective diaconal witness by the Church. It has been recognised fairly widely that such witness needs to be representative and focused through ordination, and ecumenical dialogue has endorsed the importance of the third, diaconal, order of ministry.

283   Before taking a closer look at theological reasons for these developments, the following summary is suggested:

> there is an increasing awareness amongst both laity and clergy that ministry belongs to the whole Church and not just to ordained ministers. This calls for a clearer appreciation of what it means to talk of the ministry of all Christian people. It also calls for a continuing examination of the distinctive nature of ordained ministry.

> The multiplicity of developments in the Church of England alone makes it clear that there is a real need for ministers other than priests who can exercise a general pastoral ministry in and from the Church, with its own appropriate liturgical expression. This point has been reinforced by the increasing number of candidates coming forward for ministry who do not seek priestly ministry. They do not see themselves as 'focal leaders', but rather as leading through service, with a bias to pastoral work, and a wish to minister in a supporting role.

> It is clear that existing 'recognised' categories within the Church (Church Army Officer, Reader, Accredited Lay Worker) are insufficient on their own to embody the total diaconal ministry of the Church.

> Some 700 women are now exercising a ministry as ordained deacons and some of them feel called to the diaconate as a continuing and distinctive ministry. There is also a small number of men ordained in the Church of England as distinctive deacons.

(7) THE RELATIONSHIP OF TRADITION TO CONTEMPORARY EXPERIENCE

Leadership and Service

284   Part of people's perception of the Church undoubtedly issues from their experience of, and meeting with, its public ministers, and that perception is nearly always dominated by the leadership role placed upon bishops and priests. There is a proper emphasis on the bishop as the focus of unity, leading others towards the perfect unity in God, as also on the reconciling ministry crystallised in both priest

and bishop which is expressed through their presidency of the eucharist and the sacrament of absolution. However, both of these heighten the leadership role and the servant role is obscured, since it is not focused in the public ministry of the Church. Even though bishop and priest have also been ordained deacon, the element of service is overlaid with expectations and assumptions about leadership. Yet, from the beginning, the notion of *diakonia* has been central to the Church's ministry in its call to represent Christ to his Church, and through his Church to the world. Mirroring God's nature as revealed in Christ, ministers are called to focus what should be true of the whole Church. However, leadership has received greater emphasis than servanthood, and this contributed to the protest in the 1960s by those who sought a more clearly serving Church.

285   In addition to emphasising the essential part that *diakonia* or service has to play in both the life of the Church and in its ministry, the point has already been made that the Church is called to reflect in its life the nature of God in Christ; also that the ordained ministry is called to focus God's nature in individual ministers. These represent Christ's ministry to the Church, calling that Church to its ministerial role in him and, on behalf of the Church, representing Christ to a wider community. This can be said of bishops and priests, as well as of deacons. For, as the focus of unity and 'father in God' of a diocese, the Bishop is called to represent the perfect unity of God in Christ and his fatherly care for his people. Similarly, the priest represents these elements in a smaller locality and stands on the boundary as the focus of the Church's ministry of reconciliation, so that it is appropriate that the priest should preside at the eucharist and pronounce absolution.

286   In the same way, it follows that the ordained deacon represents in a special way the diaconal nature of God in Christ to the Church and, through the Church, to the wider community. It could, of course, be argued that though the servant role is important, so too are those of the teacher and healer, as is clear both from Jesus' ministry and from the ministry of the Church. However, the argument so far rehearsed has not based ministry in the Church primarily on the ministry of Jesus as reflected in the gospel narratives, important though they are. Instead, an attempt has been made to root everything in a theological understanding of the nature of God, as revealed in Jesus Christ and as

set out in their different ways by both Paul and the evangelists. On this basis, service lies at the heart of all theology of ministry. Healing arises from it and is a sign both of that service and of the reconciliation made known in Christ; and teaching is partly effected through the example of service. But teaching in its traditional sense is more appropriately associated with the ministry of the bishop and priest, since, as individuals within the community exercising a focal leadership role, they are those upon whom the main work of teaching should fall.

Ordination and Baptism

287   Some brief mention of the significance of ordination needs to be made and the two most important factors to note are those of authorisation and empowerment. Authority has been understood in a variety of ways throughout the centuries and some of them have placed undue emphasis on status and power. Nevertheless it is important that the minister receives confidence through the authorisation of ordination and, still more, that the Church can feel confidence by this means. Richard Hanson writes that people 'must have confidence that the person who in their name calls upon God . . . is the authentic representative of the church, and not someone with no more authority, than that of an individual Christian.'[31]

288   Empowerment relates the individual's own talents and abilities to the grace of God, so that they are still used, but they are also empowered and set free through God's grace. The lesson of the priority of God's grace is one of the most important lessons for the ordained minister to learn, and never more so than in contemporary society which places great stress on competition and self-reliance. The deacon has most to teach us here through the manner of service given; empowered by God's grace, the deacon (as well as the bishop and priest) receives the confidence of the Christian community by virtue of ordination and thereby acts as a focus of the ministry of the whole Church.

289   However, whilst they focus the diaconal ministry of the Church, deacons are not called to take over that ministry, and the explosion of many kinds of diaconal ministry is to be welcomed and encouraged as a means of helping the Church more effectively to manifest its true nature. That ministry is encouraged and its growth is strengthened by deacons who are ordained to be a limited public focus on the Church's

diaconal role. Thus they parallel what is true of bishops and priests in their focusing of the Church's episcopal and priestly nature.

290   But, alongside ordination, we need to re-establish the centrality of baptism as that rite which commissions all members of the Christian community to witness to their faith and to perform their ministry, however implicitly that may be expressed in their work and daily living. It is neither desirable nor necessary to ordain as deacons all who at the present time exercise even an identifiable diaconal ministry within the Church. However, lay ministry needs encouragement and some assistance if it is to assume an effective diaconal role, and recent surveys have suggested that the Church's role as servant within the wider community comes low on the agenda of many lay people within the churches.[32] Deacons should, amongst other things, strengthen and encourage the total diaconal ministry of the Church, especially in assisting it to reach out into the wider community.

Transitional and Distinctive Diaconate

291   The question arises of the way in which the Church of England has used the diaconate until recent times. If it is to remain simply as a transitional state on the road to priesthood, it seems difficult to justify its continuing existence. Whilst it may be argued that priests and bishops remain deacons, the fact that leadership often obscures service means that their diaconal role is easily forgotten. It has thus become largely a vestigial office (until recently even more so in the Roman Catholic Church than in the Anglican Communion) and it is easy to see why the 1974 report *Deacons in the Church*[33] recommended its abolition. If the diaconate is to have any significance then it needs to exist in its own right, and Karl Rahner states this cogently: 'If the necessity and meaning of the sacramental transmission of an office must be justified by the office itself, then the office itself must have a significance in the Church which can really justify a sacramental rite'.[34] Rahner goes on from there to place this alongside other arguments in favour of restoring a distinctive or, as he rather unhappily labels it, 'absolute' diaconate.

292   It is reasonable to assume that if the Church has distinctive deacons, then that will help potential priests in their time as transitional deacons to make better sense of the order into which they are first ordained. The deacon stands as an ambassador or apostle of

the diaconal ministry of Christ and, within the Church of England, we now have substantial numbers of women fulfilling that ministry. It is important to recognise and support their ministry without prejudging in either direction the outstanding issue as to whether the Church of England should ordain women to the priesthood or not.

Being and Doing

293 In seeking how best the diaconate may be used within the contemporary world, it is necessary that it be given the sort of sacramental significance to which Rahner refers, so as to rescue it from its vestigial status. To do so is to recognise the distinctive role of ordained ministers in the life of the Church. The argument about 'being' and 'doing' in ministry has been long and often sterile, but the issues underlying it remain significant. The sort of person one is, is defined not only by one's activity, but also in one's passivity; contemplative prayer and social action are seen to be of equal importance. So, in discussing the diaconal office, to define a deacon purely by his or her 'being' is inadequate; to define it simply by function runs the risk of reducing the Church to one more human agency amongst others and, indeed, calls into question all forms of ordained ministry, whether priestly, episcopal or diaconal. Whilst function gives reality to 'being', 'being' defines the specific nature of the ordained ministry and its place within the total ministry of the Church.

294 The 1974 Report emphasised the functional role of the deacon at the expense of other considerations, so that in its discussion of the deacon's role in worship, the assumption was that 'we have . . . others who, between them, can *do* anything in worship that a deacon can'.[33] Amongst these 'others' were included deaconesses, most of whom are now ordained deacon, and the argument has become a good deal more complex by this fact alone. 'Doing' is important and helps to give shape and symbolic reality to 'being' but on its own it is insufficient.

295 Rahner discounts a purely functional discussion of the deacon's role, whilst at the same time seeing the importance of relating that role to specific tasks. He writes: 'He (effectively the minister) will in a real sense be an "ambassador", or *"apostolos"*, who by his divine mission is sent out of his own personal situation in order to carry the

gospel "in season and out of season" into strange places.'[35] This is one of the factors that marks off the deacon's ministry from the diaconal ministry of all lay people and the same argument exists when one looks towards the priesthood. Since all priests are also ordained deacon first, a purely functional model could lead us into difficulties in defining the 'diaconal' work of priests. However, the implications of the argument are clear: function must stand alongside one's being and both must relate to the theology which has already been expounded, and which is the basis of all diaconal life in the Church.

Pastoral and Liturgical Ministers

296   In considering exactly how diaconal ministry is to be expressed in today's world, both theological insights, based on the tradition, and reflection upon contemporary experience are helpful. The experience of the 1960s and the results of the questionnaire for this Report point to one important area of emphasis as being that of pastoral work and, more often than not, pastoral work in the wider community. This suggests that one pole of the deacon's ministry will be firmly established on, or beyond, the boundaries of the Church. Whether or not deacons see their ministry as explicitly evangelistic, many will prefer to see themselves as servants representing Christ through his Church to the wider community, by working with that community in various forms of welfare and social service, and encouraging other Christian laity to do likewise. It would be inappropriate to give specific examples here, for the deacon's ministry should be general, as is the case with ministerial priesthood, but individual deacons will develop their ministry in different areas of concern within the community, sometimes being attached to institutions (hospitals, hospices, etc.) rather than to parishes.

297   The other essential pole of the deacon's ministry lies within worship. This safeguards any practical community ministry from becoming purely human-centred social work. It also helps to make real the focal role that he or she as a deacon plays in representing Christ's diaconal ministry in the Church and becomes a sacramental representation of the Church's ministry of service. Neither of these two poles of community and worship denies the possibility of pastoral work *within* the local Church, but they are markers to point to the distinctive contribution that a deacon may make in focusing the Church's wider servant role.

Deacon, Priest, Bishop, Church and Community

298   There are a number of areas which require clarification within the ministry of the Church. One particular area where such clarification is important is in the relationship of priestly and diaconal ministry. At present all priests are first ordained deacon and, in the Church of England, generally remain deacon for about one year, after which they are also ordained to the priesthood. Whilst one might argue that all priests are elected from the college of deacons, this is to overstate the case as it exists at present and the step from deacon to priest has been largely automatic, except where an extended diaconate has been required for an individual by the bishop for pastoral or disciplinary reasons.

299   It was the beginning of this somewhat formal process, together with the growth in power of the college of priests, that in the fourth century produced the so-called *cursus honorum*. Indeed, the Book of Common Prayer of 1662, in the service entitled 'The Form and Manner of Making of Deacons', gives clear evidence of this continuing attitude in the prayer after communion: 'that they [the deacons] . . . may so well behave themselves in this inferior Office, that they may be found worthy to be called unto the higher Ministries in the Church.' This 'ladder of ministry' was certainly not present in the first three centuries of the Christian era where deacons held a place of equal but different significance in the Church to that of presbyters.

300   In a restored diaconate, it would be important to reclaim this 'equality with difference'. In response to this, some would maintain that the only way forward is to ordain deacon only those who are to remain deacon, and to ordain others direct to the priesthood. There are, however, certain disadvantages in this. For much can be learnt within the 'deacon's year' about the nature of ministry, and if we take seriously the fact that *diakonia* is the root word for ministry (and the arguments relating this to the ministry of Christ), then a priest's ministry will be impoverished by excluding the possibility of ordination first to the diaconate. In any case, much of a priest's ministry remains diaconal. Furthermore, where (perhaps in fairly rare cases) a 'distinctive' deacon feels a call later on to the priesthood and is ordained, that individual's position would be anomalous: some priests will have been ordained deacon first and others not. Anomalies are not in themselves convincing arguments against a particular

course of action, but in this case theological implications are also involved.

301 The above arguments suggest that we should not define deacons or their ministry by starting from the priesthood. This has sometimes been the approach adopted by Roman Catholic theologians. For example, Joseph Hornef writes: 'In the order of diaconate she (the Church) has created a limited participation in the priesthood, an office which corresponds to certain essential functions and tasks of the Church, and whose life is part of the lifestream of the Church.'[36] Such an approach presents three dangers: first is the tendency to define the Church through the priesthood; the second is to emphasise the *cursus honorum* in an extreme manner, by making the diaconate but a limited part of the priesthood; and the final danger is to ignore the theology which shows all ministry to be rooted as much in *diakonia* as in priesthood.

302 If, however, the diaconate is not to be defined through priesthood, are there not problems in allowing *diakonia* to underlie all ministry? The danger here is the opposite to that outlined above: priesthood seen as diaconal ministry with merely the addition of eucharistic presidency and the ministry of absolution. In an extreme form, this would define priesthood simply through sacramental functionalism in the celebration of the eucharist and the pronouncing of absolution. However, eucharistic presidency and the pronouncing of absolution should be seen rather as the crystallizing of the far wider priestly ministry which mirrors God's reconciling action in Christ, and which the priest focuses for the Church. Certainly it makes sense for the deacon to absorb part of the diaconal ministry at present exercised by the priest, but instead of threatening the priestly ministry, this should enhance it by releasing the priest for other work. It should also allow the Church to live out its servant role in the world more effectively through the deacon's work in the community. Priestly and diaconal ministry are not mutually threatening but rather complementary.

303 The ministries of priest and deacon are also complementary in that the deacon can release the priest to exercise the essential leadership role, delegated by the bishop. This the deacon does by offering a supportive ministry alongside the priest's ministry of leadership. Hence *diakonia,* which we translate as service, is to be understood as a ministry which can be exercised alongside either the

bishop or the priest. This has resonances with the experience of the early Church. Karl Rahner emphasises the point of this supportive role, but uses the term 'assistance' when he writes: 'In other words, the historically speaking very different functions of deacons are nevertheless of the one nature, *viz.* to help those who direct the Church, an assistance which does not usurp or replace the function of these leaders, but supports its exercise by those who actually direct the Church herself'.[37]

304   Rahner's comments are helpful, although there is danger in defining the ministry of the deacon simply as that of the priest's assistant and, also, he implies a wholly hierarchical model of the Church. Anglicanism, with its synodical mode of government, would want to affirm a collegial and organic model, in which direction is the responsibility of the entire body, with leadership focused in the bishops. This means that the deacon is not simply an assistant to the priest or bishop, but is primarily a support to, and encourager of, the laity. For it is particularly the deacon who is entrusted with the role of encouraging the diaconal ministry of the laity within the wider community.

305   From earliest times the deacon has also been associated with the bishop and his ministry. This traditional attachment of the deacon to the bishop is also of importance in reminding us of the universality of the Church, which broadens our vision beyond the limited confines of the individual parish (for example, ministry in social work, schools, industrial chaplaincy, etc.). As with the priest, the deacon's ministry is linked with that of the bishop, and vice versa. It was also the case that from earliest times the bishop had his own deacon or deacons, as part of his ministerial college. Here once again the broadly supportive role of the deacon is made clear, for not only does the deacon serve the local congregation and the wider community, but also the priest, or, in this case, the bishop. Thus is emphasised the interrelationship between the three aspects of God's reconciling activity in which the Church participates through its total ministry: Christ's priestly, diaconal and overseeing work is all one. This is demonstrated effectively through the close relationship between priesthood, diaconate and episcopate in the Church.

Part Three

A WAY AHEAD

7 The Future of the Diaconate

(1) AFFIRMING THE DIACONATE

Keep the Status Quo

306 Before deciding for the restoration of the diaconate, some mention should be made of the three options set out for the General Synod in 1977.[38] The first of these is to suggest retaining the diaconate simply as a 'temporary' ministry in which all those to be ordained to the priesthood serve a kind of apprenticeship. To accept this *status quo*, however, would be to ignore the many voices calling for a renewal of the diaconate and to take no account of the experience of other provinces of the Anglican Communion, as well as of other Churches. Moreover, it would allow the continuing proliferation of random *ad hoc* ministries without providing an ordered means of affirming diaconal ministry. In any case, the Church of England now has a large number of 'permanent' women deacons who need to be affirmed and encouraged in making the most of this ministry.

Discontinue the Diaconate

307 This last point alone makes the abolition of the diaconate difficult. Furthermore, it would seem to be inappropriate, not only in the light of early Church practice and contemporary experience, but also because of the importance for the Church of England of its place in the world-wide Church and of its continuity of tradition. At the Reformation the threefold order of bishop, priest and deacon was maintained and the Declaration of Assent which its ministers are currently required to make reads as follows:

> The Church of England is part of the One, Holy, Catholic and Apostolic Church worshipping the one true God, Father, Son and Holy Spirit. It professes the faith uniquely revealed in the Holy Scriptures and set forth in the catholic creeds, which faith the Church is called upon to proclaim afresh in each generation. Led by the Holy Spirit, it has borne witness to Christian truth in its historic formularies, the Thirty-nine Articles of Religion, the Book of Common Prayer and the Ordering of Bishops, Priests and Deacons.

308 The argument for abolishing the diaconate is not therefore

convincing. For the order belongs to the pattern of ministry in the universal Church, it is part of our own Church's inheritance and current ecumenical dialogues are affirmative of it (especially the Lima Text). Moreover, as earlier evidence has suggested, it has offered much within the ministry of the Church as a whole.

Enlarge the Diaconate

309　There are those who would like to see the diaconate as a kind of lay order and a kind of 'umbrella' under which to gather many kinds of diaconal ministries. Among them is Professor Anthony Hanson, who writes, 'Why should not all such ministers, readers, Church Army captains, deaconesses, full-time women workers, be ordained to the diaconate? There would be no need whatever that deacons should wear a clerical collar or be addressed as "Reverend". It should be an unaffectedly lay order.'[39]

310　Apart from the fact that most deaconesses have been ordained since these words were written, it is not clear that such a comprehensive category of ministry would be helpful. Some of those who are mentioned may not believe themselves called to ordination, and it seems likely that such an all-embracing diaconate (which was also envisaged in the Tiller Report)[40] would compound rather than dispel ministerial confusion. Perceptions are already blurred and the institution of an order into which people are 'ordained' whilst they remain 'lay' is certain to produce even less clarity. It is necessary either to ordain in the normal manner or not at all.

311　That being so, there will still be a place in the Church for the 'lay' ministries which have so powerfully proved their worth, be they Accredited Lay Workers, Readers or Church Army Officers and Sisters. A few Deaconesses remain and it seems unlikely that all diocesan 'Pastoral Lay Ministers' would or should be replaced by distinctive deacons.

Recover a Distinctive Diaconate

312　However, some of these may well find support and direction for their ministry through ordination, and a renewal of the diaconate could be built upon the selection, training and ordination of those who now exercise a diaconal ministry; for many of them are what Rahner calls 'anonymous deacons' already working within the Church.[41] It could be right for some Readers and Church Army personnel to seek ordination as distinctive deacons, but their doing so would mean that the remaining Readers' role as teachers and preachers would be focused more sharply[42] and that members of the Church Army would be enabled to devote themselves more clearly to evangelism. It seems likely that some Accredited Lay Workers might wish to be ordained to the diaconate, but there would remain those (and others in the future) who do not see themselves called to ordination or, for some reason, would be unwilling to contemplate it.

313   That some clarification of diaconal ministries is needed is shown by the replies to the diocesan questionnaire.[43] The experience of other Anglican Provinces and of other churches, together with the direction of the ecumenical dialogues, suggests that such clarification might be gained by the restoration of a distinctive diaconate. Tradition is thus affirmed by contemporary experience and together they provide a credible theology of 'permanent diaconate'. This calls for a visible form of *diakonia* in order to strengthen the total ministry of the Church, both to help the laity to understand their part in it and to be a witness to bishops and priests of servanthood as the basis of their vocation.

Vocation and Ordination

314   Since there is no merit in ordaining all who fulfil a diaconal role to the order of deacon with its focal, representative element, the question of vocation is a crucial one and relates as much to 'being' as to 'function'. To ordain someone is, on the human level, to invest them with privileges (such as membership of the House of Clergy etc., the civil right to solemnise marriages and exemption from jury service), and also with disabilities (such as exclusion from the House of Laity, liability to proceedings under clergy discipline measures and disqualification from election to the lower House of Parliament). It is also to invite people to offer themselves for an irreversible commitment and consecration of life. This means that for the diaconate, as for the priesthood, there needs to be as much certainty about the vocation as is possible. In particular, a vocation to the diaconate is not to be defined in terms of the priesthood, so that the deacon is seen as a substitute for the priest in certain (especially liturgical) situations. He or she is not a priest *manqué*. Although those who are called to the priesthood legitimately spend time as transitional deacons (and need to be encouraged to make the best use of their opportunities in that ministry), the use of the distinctive

diaconate as the first step towards priesthood ought not to be encouraged.

Clericalisation

315 Inasmuch as one of the functions of distinctive deacons is to support and encourage laity to move out into the wider community, the external signs of office are best avoided whenever they are inappropriate. Clerical collars, for example, are a helpful passport on occasions (such as visiting in a hospital), whereas in other situations it may be best to show a clearer solidarity with lay people. A wrong kind of clericalism is always to be avoided, especially if deacons are to be effective ministers in society. The ordination of distinctive deacons will doubtless bring some difficulties, but it will be important for the Church to identify them from the beginning and if the dangers of clericalism are recognised from the outset, it may be possible to avoid the worst of its pitfalls.

316 Even with a re-established distinctive diaconate, a fair amount of variety would remain, with new ministries coming into being, old ones dying and changes being made in those which continue. It is to be hoped, however, that the ordination of distinctive deacons would provide a kind of pattern and encouragement for varying diaconal ministries and hold them together in the way that the branch of a tree provides support and nourishment for many different leaves. Rather than provide a straitjacket for ministries, a distinctive diaconate could encourage greater flexibility rather than less and could make a positive contribution to the promotion of diverse ministries in allowing and urging the Church to respond to new needs and opportunities in society.

(2) SOME PRACTICAL ISSUES

Selection and Training

317 If the Church of England decides on the recovery of a distinctive diaconate, open to men as well as women, the House of Bishops will need to arrange for regulations for the selection, training and ministry of distinctive deacons.

ACCM will have to be asked to prepare criteria for selection for the diaconate, which will not necessarily be the same as those used for the priesthood.

Courses will need to be devised in colleges, within dioceses or on an inter-diocesan basis, for the training specifically of deacons, and more staff will be required for the purpose.

Some of the existing courses or training schemes may be suitable, or could easily be modified, but a question arises as to whether those courses devised for the training of men are equally appropriate for the training of the women who will probably form the majority of distinctive deacons.

It will be important to offer a pattern of ministerial formation for the (distinctive) diaconate which is distinct from that which is offered at present for the priesthood.

Stipendiary and Non-Stipendiary

318 It is to be hoped that distinctive deacons would be both stipendiary and non-stipendiary and that in both cases they would be as far as possible deployable wherever there is need. Positions would, of course, have to be available for those who are stipendiary, as is true at present for Church Army workers, Accredited Lay Workers and some women deacons.

Relationship to the Incumbent, the Bishop and the Church

319 It will be important that the work specification (and licence) make the distinctive deacon's position clear with regard to her or his relationship with the parish and its incumbent and/or the bishop and the diocese (especially where the deacon's ministry is in the context of a school, chaplaincy or 'secular' institution). The principle of a 'separate but equal' order needs to be safeguarded if the Church is to move away from the *cursus honorum* and a hierarchical model of ministry. Equally important will be the education of the Church, to enable clergy and people to understand and accept the role and function of distinctive deacons. Being a 'rediscovery', the first deacons will need encouragement and assistance to ensure that the best use is made of their ministry.

The Ordinal

320 Whilst the ASB Ordinal comes closer than that in the BCP to suggesting the possibility of the diaconate's being a life-long ministry, a future revision might consider whether the Bishop's statement at the beginning of The Declaration (p.344, Section 13) is an adequate description of the role of the distinctive deacon. There is no reason

why such a statement should not be applicable to the transitional deacon as well, but inasmuch as liturgy is also a primary means of education, it is important that the Ordinal should convey very clearly to candidates and congregation alike exactly what the Church believes about the ministry of deacons.

Transitional Deacons

321 As part of the process of rediscovery, those who are preparing for priesthood will need to be helped in the understanding and use of their time in the diaconate. For not only might they work subsequently with distinctive deacons, but their priestly ministry is necessarily based upon *diakonia*.

Change of Vocation

322 Mention has already been made of those who seek to transfer from the distinctive diaconate to the priesthood. Some thought needs to be given to the production of guidelines or regulations relating to this, taking special account of the situation in which women deacons at present find themselves. It should be noted that under the present regulations it is not possible to send a person who is already ordained (i.e. as a deacon) to a further ACCM selection conference.

Dress and Title

323 There has also been mention of clerical dress and its appropriateness for distinctive deacons. Experience at the time of the ordination of deaconesses suggests that some authoritative guidelines would be welcomed, as also about titles and forms of address.

324 It is important that such practical matters (some may think some of them trivial) be considered early on in the process of restoring the diaconate as a distinctive vocation, not least for the sake of those who already find themselves exercising this ministry.

8   Diaconal Ministry

325   Because the deacon's work is to serve both within the Church and within the community, and because he or she has a 'general' ministry, it is not possible to draw up a tidy and exhaustive list of the tasks which might be undertaken by a deacon. Particular circumstances will dictate what is to be done, and some specialisation or limitation in the individual's ministry will be necessary, according to her or his abilities and opportunities. However, there needs always to be openness to new possibilities which may occur and the deacon could well be the one to identify new crises and needs as they arise. For this reason, the necessary job description must be flexible enough to allow for the leading of the Spirit and to be capable of revision as appropriate. Nevertheless, it may be helpful to note in this report some of the areas of diaconal ministry, so as to keep them before the Church. It should be stressed, however, that in assigning a task to a deacon the question needs to be asked, 'In what way does this express his or her *diakonia* and how will it help the Church to be more truly diaconal?'

(1)   SERVANT TO THE COMMUNITY

326   As has been stated earlier, true diaconate is not an emasculated presbyterate and a primary reason for having distinctive deacons is to ensure that the Church takes seriously its responsibility to society. For the priest's time and energies are unavoidably spent chiefly in ministering to the Christian community, whereas the deacon's normal sphere of ministry is towards the wider community. If it is not, it is quite possible that the meaning of diaconal ministry will be lost both for deacons and for the Church. Moreover, the Church of England carries the responsibilities, as well as the privilege, of being the Church of the Nation. In addition to the entrée which this allows into so many spheres of national life, there is a great wealth of church and other buildings, often underused, all over the land which could be valuable resources for diaconal ministry.

327　The ASB Ordinal describes the deacon's work as 'to serve the Church of God, and to work with its members in caring for the poor, the needy, the sick, and all who are in trouble.' In the BCP there is a longer statement, where the deacon is 'to search for the sick, poor, and impotent people of the Parish, to intimate their estates, names, and places where they dwell, unto the Curate, that by his exhortation they may be relieved with the alms of the Parishioners, or others.' At the time when the BCP's description was written, there was no significant division between parish and community and the Church was the only agency for any kind of social service.

Social Needs

328　Although since then almost all of the Church's former welfare work has been taken over by a Welfare State, yet there are many who are in desperate need and the conclusions of *Faith in the City* suggest that there is much diaconal work for the Church to do. In introducing his Private Member's motion to General Synod, Mr Tom Dye said, '. . . when we are dealing with the most helpless section of the populace who need help most, we cannot leave it to random help. It needs organisation and officially recognised representatives of the Church sharing in this ministry. While in the rural areas there is a great need for people to preside at the Eucharist, I believe that in our cities . . . there is much more need for people who are like the deacons in the early Church.'[44] It should be an important part of the diaconal task to seek out and identify those for whom the State makes no provision, or who have failed to receive the help to which they are entitled, and to arrange for whatever assistance may be appropriate.

The Welfare State

329　Thus it could be that a deacon becomes expert in the legislation relating to Social Security, so that advice can be given on the benefits available to an individual and help offered in the completion of the necessary application forms. Legal assistance or financial advice for the newly-bereaved might also be obtained by the deacon.

330　Although there are agencies already at work in this field (such as the Citizen's Advice Bureau), the Church has a unique opportunity for penetrating into the community and unearthing the needs of people. Moreover, inasmuch as the Christian is able to recognise a brother or sister of Christ among those whom Karl Barth describes as 'the useless, insignificant, burdensome and destructive' (cf. Matt.

25. 31–46), a dimension of caring for the whole person is added to the provision of physical and material necessities. It is not uncommon for dioceses or parishes to employ social workers, and, particularly in a team or group ministry, there is much to be said for having a child welfare officer (for example) who is an ordained deacon.

Unemployment

331 The scourge of unemployment calls for diaconal ministry, not only in sensitive pastoral care, but also in seeking to help its victims to find work, perhaps by means of self-help schemes or self-employment projects. Ways could also be found of providing training for the acquisition of fresh skills during the worker's period of enforced idleness.

Caring Agencies and the Disadvantaged

332 The voluntary services which exist to help the needy might welcome some active help or participation by a deacon, for the aims of secular organisations like the Red Cross or Samaritans or Meals-on-Wheels are entirely compatible with the Church's *diakonia*. Many church people are already involved in these, as they are in the caring agencies of the State. But they could be encouraged in their offering of Christian service in having a deacon working alongside them. There are, too, particular groups of people in society who will always need more than even the best that welfare societies and the State can provide, and a deacon might make an important contribution to the special care given to those who are handicapped, addicted or in some way deprived. There is, for example, the increasing need to care for Aids patients and their families. A skill in crisis counselling would be a valuable resource which the Church could offer through deacons trained to give it.

Political or Social Action

333 In addition to relieving the symptoms of disorder in the lives of individuals and in society, the deacon and the Church should be working to remove the causes of disorder. As Karl Barth has written, 'The diaconate and Christian community become dumb dogs, and their service a serving of the ruling powers, if they are afraid to tackle at the social roots the evils by which they are confronted in detail.'[45] This may well involve political activity and protest, or the mobilisation of people into community action groups, when issues

111

such as housing, wages, redundancy, transport, health services, education and public morality are at stake. Such action would certainly upset many in the Church, but would equally encourage others whose natural sense of justice coincides with a Christian conscience. Both society and the Church need to be challenged, and perhaps the Church's approach to issues in the political, economic and social spheres would gain in credibility if there were deacons with expertise in these fields. By calling upon their knowledge the Church's well-meaning, but sometimes amateur, attempts to intervene in matters which are of great consequence for the Kingdom, but which are really beyond its grasp, could be greatly enhanced in their effectiveness.

(2) ENABLER OF THE CHURCH

334 The Church's concern with issues in society is at present focused through boards or councils of Social Responsibility and it would make good sense to have deacons associated with them in their work, where appropriate. For not only is a formidable list of diaconal tasks beyond the ability of one person to undertake, but it is expected of deacons (as it is of those who are concerned with Social Responsibility) that they will stimulate and enable others in the Church to exercise their diaconal ministry. As a Roman Catholic Joint Working Party on Pastoral Strategy states, 'Far from making the whole Church less "diaconal", the task of the deacon is to "actualise", to animate, to bring into effect, and to organise this servant character of the whole Church.[46]

Integrity

335 There are a number of ways in which the deacons can enable the Church with *diakonia*, but basic to all of them is his or her own role as a symbol of the servant ministry of Christ. This is well put in a statement from the Diocese of Melbourne:

> Deacons like priests and bishops are representative persons. Who they are is as important as what they do. By embodying the compassionate service and proclamation of Christ in their lives, deacons summon the whole Church to become diaconal, and so they lead and enable others to exercise their diaconate more clearly. As designated leaders in this ministry, deacons bring into focus and stimulate the diaconate of all believers, discerning and co-ordinating the gifts which the Spirit has distributed within the Christian community.[47]

336 To be an effective sign, the deacon must obviously exemplify personally the proper spirit of serving, since *diakonia* is as much 'caught' as it is taught. As Dr Lukas Vischer writes, 'Essential to the effectiveness of his ministry is the acceptance of the community (regional or parochial) he seeks to serve. He must have the trust of the people he serves and calls to service.'[48] So although 'the tasks which deacons can set themselves are as numerous as the needs of humanity' (Dr Vischer), the Church will ensure that those tasks which the deacon personally undertakes are of such a kind as to set an example of service, and of such a number as to leave time and energy to enable others to contribute their particular gifts of service.

Education

337 In seeking to discover and encourage gifts of *diakonia* in others and in matching gifts to needs, the deacon will need, if not the gift of discernment, at least an imaginative approach to the ministry. It would also be important to discover or arrange for appropriate courses and training opportunities for people to develop new or existing diaconal skills. Whether or not the deacon personally gives instruction would depend on her or his particular ability but such organisation would be part of the deacon's educational task. Another aspect of such education consists in making known to the Church or congregation the needs of its own members, as well as those of the world. Where a person requires help on working on some project, or an issue which demands the lobbying of MPs, or the raising of funds for families of political prisoners, the deacon may be able to mobilise the Church to help. Nor should it be thought that so materialistic an activity as fund-raising for humanitarian purposes is to be excluded from the diaconal task. Far from being 'unspiritual', money is an important indication of the Christian's commitment to the poor.

Motivation

338 With so much to do and so many opportunities for deacons to embody the *diakonia* of the Church, it needs to be stressed again that they are part of the ordered ministry of the Church, in order that all the members of the Church are enabled the more effectively to exercise their ministry. As a World Council of Churches document states

> The whole Church, with all its members, is called to brotherly service towards its neighbours. But if the Church is to fulfil this God-given task, it

113

requires a special diaconate, men and women who devote themselves in a special way to this task. They are not a substitute for the Church. They do not relieve the Church of its responsibility. The purpose of their special office is rather to open up the life of service for the whole Church. They are representatives of the Church in a sense that through their work and activity they remind people generally and members of the congregation in particular of their mission of brotherly service.[49]

(3) SERVANT WITHIN THE CHURCH

Pastoral Care

339 In addition to the service given by the deacon and the Church to the community, there are certain diaconal functions which belong more obviously to work with the congregation. Among these is pastoral care, particularly of those who are in some way disadvantaged, for example in chaplaincies to hospitals, old age homes and prisons. It could extend to the families of those to be baptised or confirmed, as well as to those who are bereaved, and it could be offered to those for whom the parish has responsibility in spite of their non-membership of the Church.

340 Pastoral care often has a practical dimension, as needs emerge for people to be helped with shopping, care of children, housework, transport to hospital, collection of pension, provision of meals, etc., and the deacon would be expected to see that such needs are met, usually using other people for the purpose. Effective pastoral care also has a value for witness in the community. As Professor G. W. H. Lampe writes about the early days of Christianity, 'This highly organised activity of the Church as a corporate body where it was caring for the sick and needy through the deacons, afforded an immense advantage to Christianity over its rivals. Paganism could not match its concern for the relief of the sick and needy'.[50]

341 As part of the pastoral care of a congregation the deacon may have an important part in encouraging fellowship and hospitality in the Church. In this case, in addition to organisation, the quality of the deacon's own family life would be significant. If appropriate, it could be valuable for her or his own home to be a resource for the task and for the deacon's own family to be an example for other families.

Administration

342 In close association with pastoring is the ministry of

administration, which was a major responsibility of deacons in the early centuries of their existence. Such administration might have the obviously pastoral element of organising visitors in the parish, not only to the needy, but also to newcomers and to those on the fringe of the Church. It could also be related to secretarial tasks for the parish or diocese or to giving personal assistance to the priest or bishop. This is still the one non-liturgical function which is performed by some deacons in the Orthodox Church. Or there could be the running of some church club, society or other institution which could appropriately be supervised by a deacon.

343   Finance was among the early deacon's responsibilities and, in addition to routine accountancy, there is sometimes required an organiser for some charitable event or organisation and the dispensing of Church funds or a special collection. Karl Barth suggests that the Christian community should encourage the diaconate in 'transforming the collections at divine service . . . into what they used to be in the early Church, namely, an action in which it consciously places itself behind those members who according to their special vocation are active in the diaconate, not just buying itself with a few coins, but itself engaging in the concrete work of the diaconate.'[51]

Specialist Ministries

344   In common with other ministers, individual deacons might have particular skills to be used in particular ministries such as healing, counselling, youth work, etc. Whilst instruction (especially in connection with baptism, confirmation and Sunday school) might be included, the deacon is not assumed to be, by virtue of the office, a teacher and preacher. For whereas the words in the ASB Ordinal at the giving of Scripture are similar for both deacon and priest, the BCP makes preaching firmly conditional upon the deacon's being 'licensed by the Bishop himself'.

(4) THE LITURGICAL MINISTRY OF DEACONS

345   With the growing awareness that serving God's world is central to the Church's mission, there is a need to express this in liturgical terms, so that the Church's ministry and liturgy are more diaconal in character. At the same time, the indifference shown by the world, combined with the secularisation of many of the Church's traditional diaconal roles (such as education, health care and social work) have

turned the Church in on itself: many church people feel more secure doing 'churchy' things.

346   A corollary of this is the clericalisation of ministries, with singers and those licensed to administer Holy Communion, as well as Readers, robed and occupying a designated place in the assembly which looks as if it has more to do with status than with function, let alone order. This has not helped us to be clear about what is an appropriate liturgical ministry for those in the Order of Deacons.

347   A secondary factor which confuses the position is that some still understand the diaconate not as a full and distinct Order but as a priesthood *manqué*. Some deacons are not concerned to explore the nature of diaconal ministry so much as to do everything they legally can of what a priest does, ignoring the riches of their distinctive vocation and their complementary nature in the liturgical assembly.

348   Many of the models of the Church and its ministry are structural and salvationist: the Ark, with its ministry of rescue; the Temple, contrasted with the Tabernacle, with its exclusive structure; the sacrificial priesthood, offering sacrifices on behalf of, or instead of, the people. These are images of distance, drawn from the Old Testament, and it is so often these which are evident as the norms for the life of the Church and the priesthood. But Christ's incarnate ministry stresses that gracious movement from God to man (John 1.14); the abandonment of status and structure (Phil. 2.7); 'I am among you as one who serves' (Luke 22.27). But the movement is not one way: Christ shared our poverty that we might share his riches (2 Cor. 8.9) and the same Christ who humbled himself, God has exalted (Phil. 2.9). At the heart of all ministry, including that of the deacon, is this sense of movement, of exchange; of a dynamic movement between God and humanity.

349   Liturgy, then, needs to express not only the relationship between God and his people, but also their life and mission within the wider community. Thus it serves an educational function and this demands that the deacon's part within it should communicate accurately, in word, movement and action, what the Church understands by diaconal ministry. So the deacon is primarily the servant of the assembly, focusing the servant ministry of the whole Church, and enabling the assembly to be united in the celebration. The deacon is not merely an assistant to the president.

116

350 The deacon is 'among you as one who serves'. The incarnational nature of Christ's ministry among his people is best expressed when the deacon is (where possible physically) among the worshipping community, rather than speaking at them. The deacon in the Orthodox tradition, who comes frequently among the people to lead their litanies, is a better model than the deacon who is (in the terminology of the Tridentine High Mass) one of the 'three sacred ministers' in the sanctuary.

351 If the distinctive ministry of the deacon is recognised in the Eucharist, the president is freed from a confusing multiplicity of roles and functions: of having to represent both local particularity and universal detachment, both the immediate incarnational concerns and the broader perspectives of the Kingdom which are difficult to balance. The local and immediate needs of God's people meet the universal and timeless challenge of his Gospel, represented by the apostolic authority delegated to the president by the bishop. The deacon is at the point of appropriation and interchange and symbolises in his or her movement between the people and the altar the union of the whole worshipping community. Furthermore, the work of the deacon (and all who work with her or him) in the community is firmly rooted in, and supported by, the liturgy of the Church.

9 Conclusion

352 At the end of this Report the recommendation is made that the Church of England make provision for, and encourage, men and women to serve in an ordained distinctive diaconate.

353 This conclusion is drawn from a consideration of Scripture, tradition and contemporary experience which would seem to complement and affirm one another. Furthermore, the future ministry of the Church will be greatly enriched by the restoration of a diaconate after the model and pattern of Christ's diaconate. He came 'not to be served but to serve, and to give his life as a ransom for many' (Mark 10.45), to provide an example and support for the diaconal ministry of all – laity, presbyters and bishops. All who follow him are called to be 'servants for Jesus' sake' (2 Cor. 4.5).

APPENDICES
AND
REFERENCES

Appendix 1

DISTINCTIVE (PERMANENT) DEACONS
IN THE ANGLICAN COMMUNION

	Date	Men	Women	Total	In Training
Australia	May 1987	c.10	40	c.50	c.20
Canada	Aug. 1986	38	9	47	2
England	June 1987	c.13	750	763	149
Southern Africa	July 1986	13	1	14	17
ECUSA	Aug. 1986	633	263	896	353
Scotland	Dec. 1986	–	c.17	c.17	–
Ireland	Aug. 1986	–	1	1	2
New Zealand	Aug. 1986	1	–	1	–
Wales	July 1986	–	c.20	c.20	–
TOTAL		708	1101	1808	543

Appendix 2

SPECIMEN QUESTIONNAIRE

(Identical, other than the heading, for each category of ministry)

House of Bishops –
Report on Theology of the Permanent Diaconate

PASTORAL LAY MINISTERS
(i.e. those who are part of a *diocesan* scheme for licensed/authorised
pastoral assistance, such as Lay Pastors, Pastoral Auxiliaries, Elders,
Pastoral Assistants, etc.)

1.   Name of Diocese .... (And Area ....)
(NB Please tick (√) box except where another instruction is given)   **FOR
                                                                     COMPUTER
                                                                     USE ONLY**

2.   How many Pastoral Lay Ministers do you have? (give number)

    2.1   Male Stipendiary ☐ ☐

    2.2   Male Non-stipendiary ☐ ☐

    2.3   Male Local non-stipendiary ☐ ☐

    2.4   Female Stipendiary ☐ ☐

    2.5   Female Non-stipendiary ☐ ☐

    2.6   Female Local non-stipendiary ☐ ☐

3.   *How are they selected?*

    3.1   Nationally (through ACCM) ☐ ☐

124

3.2 By your diocese acting alone
(Indicate how)

☐ ☐

    3.2.1 By interview with a selection panel

☐ ☐

    3.2.2 By individual interviews (with whom?)

☐ ☐

    3.2.3 By a variety of methods, including
         group work (give details)

☐ ☐

    3.2.4 By some other method (give details)

☐ ☐

3.3 By some other authority or agency (e.g.
Church Army, deanery, parish) (give details)

☐ ☐

    3.3.1 Which authority or agency?

☐ ☐

    3.3.2 By what method?

☐ ☐

4.1 *How are they trained?*

    4.1.1 By a theological college on a course
         recognised nationally by the House of
         Bishops

☐ ☐

    4.1.2 By a theological college on a course
         devised by the college or diocese
         (give details)

☐ ☐

    4.1.3 By a non-residential ministerial training
         scheme recognised nationally by the
         House of Bishops

☐ ☐

4.1.4 By another nationally recognised course
(e.g. General Readers' Certificate, etc.)

4.1.5 By a course devised by the diocese,
including group and/or lecture material
(give details)

4.1.6 By an individual tutorial system
(give details)

4.2 *How long is their expected training period?*
(give number of academic years)

4.3 *How is their training funded?*

4.3.1 By central Church of England funds

4.3.2 By diocesan funds

4.3.3 By parochial funds

4.3.4 By the student

4.3.5 By other means (give details)

5.1 *What is the nature of their licence or authorisation?*

5.1.1 To the diocese

5.1.2. To the deanery

5.1.3 To the parish

□ □

5.1.4   Other (give details)

5.2   *What is the period of their licence or authorisation?*

5.2.1   Indefinite   □ □

5.2.2   A limited period (give details)   □ □

5.2.3   Other (give details)   □ □

6.   *What does the diocese see as focus of work?*
Either
6.1   General Ministry (including pastoral care,
      teaching, preaching, liturgical duties, etc.)   □ □

Or
6.2   Specialised ministry (tick as many boxes as
      are appropriate)   □ □

6.2.1   Pre- and post-baptismal care   □ □

6.2.2   Care of the bereaved   □ □

6.2.3   Marriage preparation   □ □

6.2.4   Ministry to the sick   □ □

6.2.5   Counselling   □ □

6.2.6   Teaching (e.g. Sunday School, baptism
        and confirmation preparation, study
        groups, etc.)   □ □

6.2.7   Preaching

6.2.8   Liturgical duties

6.2.9   Administration

6.2.10 Children and young people

6.2.11 The wider community (e.g.
        involvement in caring organisations,
        trades unions, other social concerns,
        etc.)

6.2.12 Other specialised ministry
        (give details)

7. It would be a great help to have a very brief description of how you
    see their rôle in general terms.

THANK YOU!

The Bishop of Portsmouth
Bishopswood,
FAREHAM, Hampshire PO14 1NT.

Appendix 3

ACCREDITED LAY WORKERS

	MALE				FEMALE				
	S	NSM	LNSM	TOTAL MALE	S	NSM	LNSM	TOTAL FEMALE	TOTAL
Bath & Wells	1			1	1			1	2
Birmingham						2	1	3	3
Blackburn					1	2		3	3
Bradford	1			1	2			2	3
Bristol	1			1					1
Canterbury	1			1					1
Carlisle						2		2	2
Chelmsford	1			1	1	1		2	3
Chester					2			2	2
Chichester	2			2	5	3		8	10
Coventry	1			1	2	1		3	4
Derby						1	2	3	3
Durham					5	1		6	6
Ely									
Europe									
Exeter						1		1	1
Gloucester					3			3	3
Guildford									
Hereford						1		1	1
Leicester					3	2		5	5
Lichfield	1			1	4	6		10	11
Lincoln	3			3	5	1		6	9
Liverpool					2	1		3	3
London/London area									
London/Edmonton					3			3	3
London/Kensington									
London/Stepney					1			1	1
London/Willesden	2			2	1			1	3
Manchester					3			3	3
Newcastle	1			1	3	1		4	5
Norwich						1		1	1
Oxford					2	3		5	5

DEACONS IN THE MINISTRY OF THE CHURCH

	MALE				FEMALE				
	S	NSM	LNSM	TOTAL MALE	S	NSM	LNSM	TOTAL FEMALE	TOTAL
Peterborough	1			1	2	3		5	6
Portsmouth						2		2	2
Ripon									
Rochester	1		1	2	3			3	5
St. Albans		1		1	3	4		7	8
St. Edmundsbury & Ipswich	1			1		2		2	3
Salisbury/Ramsbury					2	1		3	3
Salisbury/Sherborne					1			1	1
Sheffield	1			1	2	2		4	5
Sodor & Man									
Southwark					4	5		9	9
Southwell					1			1	1
Truro						2		2	2
Wakefield						2		2	2
Winchester	1			1		3		3	4
Worcester						1		1	1
York	1			1	3	1		4	5
	21	1	1	23	71	57	3	131	154

DEACONESSES

	S	NSM	LNSM	TOTAL
Bath & Wells	1	7		8
Birmingham	11	9		20
Blackburn	1	2		3
Bradford	8	3		11
Bristol	20	15		35
Canterbury	9	4		13
Carlisle	4	1		5
Chelmsford	11	25		36
Chester	7	7		14
Chichester	7	10		17
Coventry	10	5		15

	S	NSM	LNSM	TOTAL
Derby	12	4		16
Durham	1	1		2
Ely	8	5		13
Europe	1	1		2
Exeter	4	13		17
Gloucester	5	3		8
Guildford	9			9
Hereford	3	3		6
Leicester	7	6		13
Lichfield	20	5		25
Lincoln	18	7		25
Liverpool	20	1		21
London/London area	1			1
London/Edmonton	3	3		6
London/Kensington	15	15		30
London/Stepney	11	2	2	15
London/Willesden	11	2		13
Manchester	17	3		20
Newcastle	4	3		7
Norwich	7	6		13
Oxford	23	8		31
Peterborough	1			1
Portsmouth	7	7		14
Ripon	10	2		12
Rochester	11	14		25
St. Albans	19	34		53
St. Edmundsbury & Ipswich	3	2		5
Salisbury/Ramsbury	2	8		10
Salisbury/Sherborne	7	6		13
Sheffield	13	3		16
Sodor & Man				
Southwark	29	18		47
Southwell	16	8		24
Truro	1	3		4
Wakefield	6	3		9
Winchester	5			5
Worcester	12	6		18
York	17	2		19
TOTAL	448	295	2	745

CHURCH ARMY

	MALE				FEMALE				
	S	NSM	LNSM	TOTAL MALE	S	NSM	LNSM	TOTAL FEMALE	TOTAL
Bath & Wells									
Birmingham	3			3	2			2	5
Blackburn	3			3	1			1	4
Bradford	1			1					1
Bristol	2	2		4	2			2	6
Canterbury	2			2					2
Carlisle	1			1	1	2		3	4
Chelmsford	5			5	3			3	8
Chester	2			2					2
Chichester	9	1		10					10
Coventry	2			2		1		1	3
Derby	4			4		1		1	5
Durham	7	1		8	1			1	9
Ely	1			1	1			1	2
Europe									
Exeter	5			5	1			1	6
Gloucester	3			3	1			1	4
Guildford	4			4					4
Hereford									
Leicester	1			1					1
Lichfield	2			2	2	1		3	5
Lincoln	1			1					1
Liverpool	7			7	5			5	12
London/London area	1			1					1
London/Edmonton	1			1					1
London/Kensington	1			1					1
London/Stepney	1			1	1			1	2
London/Willesden	2			2	2	1		3	5
Manchester									
Newcastle	1			1	2			2	3
Norwich	5			5					5
Oxford	9			9	5			5	14
Peterborough									
Portsmouth	4			4					4
Ripon	1	1		2	3			3	5
Rochester		2		2	1			1	3
St. Albans	4	2		6	1	2		3	9

	MALE				FEMALE				
				TOTAL				TOTAL	
	S	NSM	LNSM	MALE	S	NSM	LNSM	FEMALE	TOTAL
St. Edmundsbury & Ipswich	4			4	2			2	6
Salisbury/Ramsbury						1		1	1
Salisbury/Sherborne									
Sheffield	2			2					2
Sodor & Man									
Southwark	9	5		14	3	3		6	20
Southwell	2			2					2
Truro	1			1					1
Wakefield	1			1	1			1	2
Winchester	3			3					3
Worcester	3			3					3
York	5			5		1		1	6
TOTAL	125	14	0	139	41	13	0	54	193

READERS

	MALE				FEMALE				
				TOTAL				TOTAL	
	S	NSM	LNSM	MALE	S	NSM	LNSM	FEMALE	TOTAL
Bath & Wells	217			217	27			27	244
Birmingham	138			138	35			35	173
Blackburn	124			124	24			24	148
Bradford	74			74	12			12	86
Bristol	93			93	22			22	115
Canterbury	142			142	50			50	192
Carlisle	96			96	29			29	125
Chelmsford	196			196	29			29	225
Chester	262			262	49			49	311
Chichester	210			210	41			41	251
Coventry	122			122	26			26	148
Derby	141			141	48			48	189

DEACONS IN THE MINISTRY OF THE CHURCH

| | MALE | | | | FEMALE | | | | |
	S	NSM	LNSM	TOTAL MALE	S	NSM	LNSM	TOTAL FEMALE	TOTAL
Durham		119		119	21			21	140
Ely		71		71	20			20	91
Europe			42	42			4	4	46
Exeter	1	167		168	27			27	195
Gloucester		134		134	18			18	152
Guildford		107		107	18			18	125
Hereford		72		72	8			8	80
Leicester		132		132	23			23	155
Lichfield			265	265			61	61	326
Lincoln		96		96	13			13	109
Liverpool		194		194	35			35	229
London/London area		12		12	1			1	13
London/Edmonton			34	34			6	6	40
London/Kensington		38		38	5			5	43
London/Stepney		14		14	2			2	16
London/Willesden		47		47	7			7	54
Manchester		200		200	32			32	232
Newcastle		87		87	20			20	107
Norwich		171		171	51			51	222
Oxford		183		183	43			43	226
Peterborough		65		65	10			10	75
Portsmouth			56	56			17	17	73
Ripon		70		70	25			25	95
Rochester			188	188			43	43	231
St. Albans		172		172	25			25	197
St. Edmundsbury & Ipswich		177		177	35			35	212
Salisbury/Ramsbury		67		67	10			10	77
Salisbury/Sherborne		175		175	25			25	200
Sheffield		70		70	13			13	83
Sodor & Man			17	17	2			2	19
Southwark		300		300	76			76	376
Southwell		192		192	44			44	236
Truro		76		76	9			9	85
Wakefield		99		99	29			29	128
Winchester		19	116	135	16		30	46	181
Worcester		102		102	18			18	120
York	2	150		152	44			44	196
TOTAL	3	5393	718	6114	1117	161		1278	7392

DISTINCTIVE DEACONS

		MALE		TOTAL
	S	NSM	LNSM	MALE
Bath & Wells				
Birmingham	1			1
Blackburn				
Bradford		1		1
Bristol				
Canterbury				
Carlisle				
Chelmsford				
Chester				
Chichester				
Coventry				
Derby				
Durham				
Ely				
Europe				
Exeter				
Gloucester				
Guildford				
Hereford				
Leicester				
Lichfield				
Lincoln				
Liverpool				
London/London area				
London/Edmonton				
London/Kensington				
London/Stepney				
London/Willesden				
Manchester	1			1
Newcastle				
Norwich				
Oxford		1		1
Peterborough				
Portsmouth		7		7
Ripon				
Rochester				
St. Albans		2		2

		MALE		TOTAL
	S	NSM	LNSM	MALE
St. Edmundsbury & Ipswich				
Salisbury/Ramsbury				
Salisbury/Sherborne				
Sheffield		1		1
Sodor & Man				
Southwark				
Southwell				
Truro				
Wakefield				
Winchester				
Worcester				
York				
TOTAL	2	12		14

PASTORAL LAY MINISTERS

	MALE			TOTAL	FEMALE			TOTAL	
	S	NSM	LNSM	MALE	S	NSM	LNSM	FEMALE	TOTAL
Bath & Wells			14	14	1		9	10	24
Birmingham									
Blackburn			18	18			73	73	91
Bradford									
Bristol									
Canterbury									
Carlisle			18	18			18	18	36
Chelmsford									
Chester						3		3	3
Chichester									
Coventry									
Derby						1	2	3	3

	MALE			FEMALE			
	S NSM	LNSM	TOTAL MALE	S NSM	LNSM	TOTAL FEMALE	TOTAL
Durham							
Ely		30	30		32	32	62
Europe							
Exeter							
Gloucester							
Guildford		94	94		250	250	344
Hereford							
Leicester					27	27	27
Lichfield							
Lincoln		15	15		38	38	53
Liverpool							
London/London area				1		1	1
London/Edmonton							
London/Kensington							
London/Stepney	1		1	4		4	5
London/Willesden							
Manchester							
Newcastle							
Norwich							
Oxford							
Peterborough							
Portsmouth					1	1	1
Ripon							
Rochester		7	7	60		60	67
St. Albans	18		18	1 14		15	33
St. Edmundsbury & Ipswich		117	117		96	96	213
Salisbury/Ramsbury		59	59		118	118	177
Salisbury/Sherborne		93	93		187	187	280
Sheffield		4	4		7	7	11
Sodor & Man							
Southwark		13	13		80	80	93
Southwell							
Truro							
Wakefield		153	153		322	322	475
Winchester		100	100		300	300	400
Worcester							
York		3	3		4	4	7
TOTAL	19	738	757	4 81	1564	1649	2406

Appendix 4

STATISTICS FROM CHURCH ARMY HEADQUARTERS

Distribution of Church Army Officers within each Diocese

DIOCESE	DIV. OF EVANGELISM	DIV. OF SOCIAL RESPONSIBILITY	HEADQUARTERS* (includes Appeals Dept.)	TOTAL
Bath & Wells	1	–	–	1
Birmingham	8	–	–	8
Blackburn	6	–	–	6
Bradford	2	–	–	2
Bristol	6	–	–	6
Canterbury	4	–	–	4
Carlisle	3	1	–	4
Chelmsford	17	2	–	19
Chester	2	–	–	2
Chichester	10	2	1	13
Coventry	5	–	–	5
Derby	4	3	–	7
Durham	9	1	–	10
Ely	1	1	–	2
Exeter	6	3	–	9
Gloucester	3	1	–	4
Guildford	2	2	–	4
Hereford	–	–	–	–
Leicester	3	–	–	3
Lichfield	8	–	–	8
Lincoln	1	–	–	1
Liverpool	10	3	1	14
London	10	16	2	28
Manchester	8	2	1	11
Newcastle	3	–	–	3
Norwich	5	1	–	6
Oxford	11	1	5	17
Peterborough	–	–	–	–
Portsmouth	3	2	–	5
Ripon	5	1	–	6
Rochester	4	1	1	6

Distribution of Church Army Officers within each Diocese

DIOCESE	DIV. OF EVANGELISM	DIV. OF SOCIAL RESPONSIBILITY	HEADQUARTERS* (includes Appeals Dept.)	TOTAL
St. Albans	7	1	–	8
St. Edmundsbury & Ipswich	10	–	–	10
Salisbury	2	–	2	4
Sheffield	2	–	–	2
Sodor & Man	–	–	–	–
Southwark	21	7	13	41

* Training College and Counselling

DIOCESE	DIV. OF EVANGELISM	DIV. OF SOCIAL RESPONSIBILITY	HEADQUARTERS* (includes Appeals Dept.)	TOTAL
Southwell	1	3	1	5
Truro	1	–	–	1
Wakefield	3	–	1	4
Winchester	6	–	–	6
Worcester	4	–	–	4
York	5	5	–	10
Germany	8	–	–	8
Wales	2	4	–	6
N. Ireland	12	–	–	12
Eire	3	–	–	3
Scotland	4	–	–	4
Seconded overseas	5	–	–	5
			TOTAL	347

11 Captains are ordained.
6 Sisters are deaconesses.

ACTIVE OFFICERS OF THE SOCIETY
AS AT 27th OCTOBER 1986

DEPARTMENT	PAID BY CA	EMPLOYED BY OUTSIDE AGENCIES*	UNEMPLOYED WIVES	TOTAL
Evangelism (North)	9	48	5	62
Evangelism (South)	7	81	10	98
Evangelism (Ireland)	7	6	2	15
Evangelism (Others)	6	1	2	9
Director of Evangelism	1	—	—	1
Overseas	1	4	—	5
Youth	7	25	1	33
Chaplaincies & Forces	20	15	2	37
Social Responsibility	34	31	1	66
Training Division	9	—	1	10
O's not covered by Divisional Lists	3	—	—	3
PR & Appeals	4	1	—	5
Counselling	3	—	—	3
TOTAL	111	212	24	347

* These figures include officers on leave of absence, sabbatical and further training.

Appendix 5

A NOTE ON CHURCH SOCIAL WORKERS

Although brief mention was made of Church Social Workers in the section on Women's Ministry in this Report (para. 48), Social Work was not a category included in the Questionnaire sent to dioceses (see para. 161). Because much of the work undertaken by Social Workers is diaconal in its nature, there follows a note on the numbers and deployment of Social Workers in the Church of England, based on information supplied by Alison Webster (Secretary of the Social Policy Committee of the Board for Social Responsibility). A full picture would need to include the Church of England Children's Society, the Girls' Friendly Society, the Church Housing Association and other caring agencies.

About half of the dioceses employ Social Workers, of which London (with 48 full-time and 35 part-time workers) and Southwark (16 full-time and 15 part-time) have the most. Other dioceses employ on average between two and six workers, with perhaps another three or four per residential project. There is no central register but an estimate suggests that there are at least 200 full-time workers and between 50 and 70 part-time workers, spread between field, residential and community workers who are employed by Boards of Social Responsibility and diocesan agencies. There are also people who offer administrative support (and of London's 35 part-time workers 17 are administrative).

There is a great variety of work undertaken and each diocese has made independent decisions about social work provision in the light of local needs, diocesan commitment, other demands and the historical inheritance of the agencies involved. Thus generalisations are difficult. However, the general trend is away from psychodynamically based work with single parents (in the Moral Welfare tradition) to group work, family work, community work and the continuing of some residential work.

Most bishops authorise workers for their work, usually in a special service, although some dioceses do not appear always to 'own' the work fully. Thus, many value the support of a strong network of senior Social Workers who meet in Church House three times a year for the sharing of information and discussion of policy, as well as consideration of matters of common concern such as recruitment and training, priorities and fund-raising. Social Workers are also being encouraged to join the newly established Anglican Association for Social Reponsibility and they are well represented on its executive. The purpose of this Association is 'to provide education, training and support for those employed by social responsibility agencies in the Anglican Communion in the United Kingdom, and to advance education and action in the churches and in the community on matters of social justice and welfare'. Authorised Social Workers are involved in: adoption agencies, work with single parents and families, residential care, community work, family life education, student training, counselling (especially bereavement and drug counselling schemes), conciliation projects, care of the disabled and the support of community care groups. *Faith in the City* provides additional challenges with its implications for diocesan Social Workers in the future.

References

[1] General Synod, House of Bishops' Minutes, 22nd January 1986, 10.

[2] General Synod, Report of Proceedings, July 1981, p.629.

[3] *Women in Ministry:* The Report of a Working Party on Women's Ministry, set up by the Ministry Committee of ACCM and the Council for Women's Ministry in the Church, 1968, p.40.

[4] *ACCM/CIO* 1974.

[5] General Synod, GS 344, pp.24–5.

[6] *Lambeth Conference 1968: Preliminary Information*, p.109.

[7] *The Lambeth Conference 1968* (Report), p.105 (cf. *The Lambeth Conference 1958*, Resolution 88, p.1.50).

[8] *ACC 3*, pp.41–4.

[9] *ACC 6*, pp.77–8.

[10] In this section use is made of Janet Grierson's *The Deaconess* (CIO 1981) and *Women in Ministry: A Study* (The Report of a Working Party on Women's Ministry set up by the Ministry Committee of ACCM and the Council for Women's Ministry in the Church in 1968); also Dame Christian Howard's paper *Women's Ministry – Lay Ministry 1947–1979.*

[11] Letter from L. E. Sheneman, Executive Director, LCA, Division of Professional Leadership.

[12] *Self-Supporting Presbyters and Deacons in the Methodist Church of New Zealand*, Committee on Ministry, 1984, p.12.

[13] See Appendix 1 for statistics of Distinctive Deacons in the Anglican Communion.

[14] *The Episcopal Church Annual 1987*. 1985: 2,972,607; 1984: 3,004,758. For communicants, 1985: 1,881,250 (domestic); 82,375 (overseas).

[15] In this section much use is made of a submission to the Commission considering the restoration of the diaconate in the CPSA, 'The Need for a Restoration of the Diaconate', 1981.

[16] In this section use is made of a paper from the Doctrine Committee of the SEC, 'A Distinctive or Permanent Diaconate of Men and Women'.

[17] Reference is made in this section to *Baptism, Eucharist and Ministry*, World Council of Churches, Geneva 1982; *The Final Report* of the Anglican–Roman Catholic International Commission, CTS/SPCK, London 1982; *God's Reign and Our Unity*, SPCK/Saint Andrew Press, London/Edinburgh 1984.

[18] See also para. 29.

[19] *We Believe in God*: A Report by the Doctrine Commission of the General Synod of the Church of England, London 1987, p.70.

[20] R. C. Moberly, *Ministerial Priesthood*, London 1910.

[21] Lady (Helen) Oppenheimer, in *Stewards of the Mysteries of God* (ed. Eric James), London 1979, pp.11–21.

[22] Stephen Bayne, *Now is the Accepted Time*, Cincinnati 1983.

[23] A. T. Hanson, *The Pioneer Ministry*, London 1961.

[24] M. Santer, 'Diaconate and Discipleship', *Theology*, May 1978, pp.179–82.

[25] Charles Gore, *The Incarnation of the Son of God*, London 1891.

[26] J. Moltmann, *The Crucified God*, E.T. London 1974; and J. Moltmann, *The Trinity and Kingdom of God*, E.T. London 1981. See also G. Studdert-Kennedy in his poems *The Unutterable Beauty* and another book *The Hardest Part*.

[27] *We Believe in God*: A report by the Doctrine Commission of the General Synod of the Church of England, London 1987, p.159.

[28] W. H. Vanstone, *Love's Endeavour, Love's Expense*. London 1977, p.58.

[29] W. H. Vanstone, ibid., p.115.

[30] cf. A. Dulles, *Models of the Church*, Dublin 1976, esp. pp.83ff.

[31] R. P. C. Hanson, *Christian Priesthood Examined*, London 1979, pp.108–9.

[32] *Views from the Pews: Lent 1986*. British Council of Churches, London 1986.

[33] *Deacons in the Church*, ACCM/CIO, London 1974.

[34] K. Rahner, *Theological Investigations*, Vol. 5, E.T. London 1966.

[35] K. Rahner, op.cit., p.300.

[36] J. Hornef, *The New Vocation*, E.T. Cork 1963, p.17.

[37] K. Rahner, op.cit., p.270.

[38] See Introduction, p.1 above.

[39] A. T. Hanson, *Church, Sacraments and Ministry*, London 1975, p.107.

[40] J. Tiller, *A Strategy for the Church's Ministry*, London 1983.

[41] K. Rahner, op.cit., p.277.

[42] This point has been emphasised in the recent report on Reader training: 'The Ministry and Training of Readers in the Church of England: a Report of a Warden's Working Group', ACCM, London, October 1986.

[43] See Chapter 4, p.51 ff.

[44] General Synod, *Report of Proceedings*; July 1981, p.631.

[45] Karl Barth, *Church Dogmatics*, T. & T. Clark 1962, IV.3.2, p.893.

[46] Catholic Information Office, *The Church 2000*, quoted in GS 344, p.6.

[47] Melbourne Diocesan Diaconate Committee, *The Distinctive Diaconate*, May 1985. Quoted by Dcn Sister Teresa, CSA, in *The Diaconate and the Laity*, Study 24 of Distinctive Diaconate, June 1986.

[48] Lukas Vischer, *The Ministry of Deacons*, WCC 1965, quoted in GS 344, p.19.

[49] WCC, World Church Studies No. 4, *The Deaconess*, Geneva 1965, p.10.

[50] Quoted from *Essays in Honour of Karl Barth* by Mr T. L. Dye in General Synod, *Report of Proceedings*, November 1977, p.1115.

[51] Karl Barth, op.cit., p.894.

Note: Literature on the diaconate is extensive, but in addition to the publications noted above and in the text of the Report, special mention should be made of James M. Barnett, *The Diaconate*, Seabury, New York 1981.